19.8

why arendt matters

May 1, 1972

Jill Krementz

Elisabeth
Young-Bruehl
Why Arendt
Matters

yale university press   new haven & london

Frontispiece: Hannah Arendt, photographed by Jill Krementz, from *Portraits: Series of Photographs in Arendt's Apartment, May 1, 1972.* Courtesy the Hannah Arendt Blücher Literary Trust.

Designed by Nancy Ovedovitz and set in Adobe Garamond by Integrated Publishing Solutions. Printed in the United States of America.

Library of Congress Cataloging-in-Publication Data
Young-Bruehl, Elisabeth.
Why Arendt matters / Elisabeth Young-Bruehl.
p. cm.—(Why X matters)
Includes bibliographical references and index.
ISBN-13: 978-0-300-12044-8 (alk. paper)
ISBN-10: 0-300-12044-3 (alk. paper)
1. Arendt, Hannah—Political and social views. 2. Political science—Philosophy. 3. Totalitarianism. I. Title.
JC251.A74Y69 2006
320.5092—dc22   2006018235

A catalogue record for this book is available from the British Library.

The paper in this book meets the guidelines for permanence and durability of the Committee on Production Guidelines for Book Longevity of the Council on Library Resources.

10 9 8 7 6 5 4 3 2 1

Also by Elisabeth Young-Bruehl

Freedom and Karl Jaspers's Philosophy
Hannah Arendt: For Love of the World
Vigil (a novel)
Anna Freud: A Biography
Mind and the Body Politic: Essays, 1975–1987
Freud on Women (editor)
Global Cultures (editor)
The Anatomy of Prejudices
*Subject to Biography: Psychoanalysis, Feminism,
    and Writing Women's Lives*
Cherishment: A Psychology of the Heart (with
    Faith Bethelard)
Where Do We Fall When We Fall in Love?

contents

introduction

"The banality of evil." That is the sound bite by which Hannah Arendt has become popularly known. A political theorist and philosopher who before her death in 1975 had written more than a dozen dense volumes, several of them masterpieces of political analysis, and who since her death has been the subject of hundreds of books and articles, lives on in newspeak through just four words. In and of itself, or even sitting in the subtitle of her *Eichmann in Jerusalem: A Report on the Banality of Evil,* the phrase is full of suggestion and portent, but without interpretation it signifies nothing.

What do people make of it when, every time some especially appalling, hard-to-fathom mass crime takes place, "the banality of evil" turns up in their morning papers or jumps out of the mouths of TV pundits? Recently, the *New York Times* Week in Review ran front-page pictures of the Nazi Adolf Eichmann at his 1961 trial and Saddam Hussein at his current trial under the caption "From Banality to Audacity." In the accompanying story,

Arendt's phrase was predictably and reverently invoked—and completely misunderstood.

In common parlance, the abstract noun *evil* hardly needs an adjective, any more than *good* needs one. What *does* the noun *banality* suggest when coupled with *evil*? Superficial, ordinary, dull, trivial—aren't these qualities of persons, not characteristics of evil?

To understand what Hannah Arendt herself meant by "the banality of evil" requires a little acquaintance with Immanuel Kant, the Enlightenment sage of Königsberg (now Kaliningrad), the city on the Baltic Sea in what was then East Prussia and is now Russia, where Arendt herself was born in 1906 and lived until she became a university student. For Kant, the abstract noun *evil* does sometimes need an adjective: *radical*. Radical evil is that type of evil, in Kant's view, which is rooted in (has its *radix* in) an evil motivation, an intention to do evil, a person's evil heart. Kant held radical evil to be rare and quite different from evil that is done out of ignorance or an intention to do good that has gone awry. In her early writings, Arendt had adopted this phrase of Kant's as she tried to think about the Nazi concentration camps, "factories of death" as she called them. Such an invention, she felt then, could have come only from an intention to do evil, to achieve some end outside of commonsense reasoning. A factory designed for systematically stripping human beings of their humanity and then reducing them to ash could not serve any rational war effort or economic plan.

After she attended his 1961 trial in Jerusalem, and saw Eichmann in the flesh, speaking his strange bureaucrat's German,

Arendt concluded that he was a superficial person, thoroughly conformist to his thoroughly banal society, with no independent sense of responsibility, motivated only by a wish to move up in the Nazi hierarchy. Crucially, he was "thoughtless," by which she meant not careless but without common sense or the ability to think. He could recite moral rules; he could even, when asked, recite Kant's famous categorical imperative, which stipulates that one should not follow a rule that one would be unwilling to have as a rule for everyone. But Eichmann could neither ask himself nor think through the question that Arendt considered essential to moral *experience,* one that she (very provocatively) held was not at all a matter of following rules: "Could I live with myself if I did this deed?"

In her report on Eichmann's trial, Arendt provided no analysis of how he came to be a thoughtless person nor any reflection on moral experience generally, although from his testimony she identified the moment when Eichmann crucially did not think but just went along: four weeks after the head of the S.S. intelligence service, Reinhardt Heydrich, informed him, on July 31, 1941, that a Final Solution of the Jewish question—that is, extermination of the Jews—had become official policy. During those four weeks, Eichmann had opportunities to observe firsthand the grisly preliminary killing operations in Poland, and he was repelled by them. But after that period he assumed his responsibilities for transporting Jews to just the kind of deaths that had so repelled him. As Arendt remarked: "It is of great political interest to know how long it takes an average person to overcome his innate repugnance toward crime, and what exactly happens to him once he has reached that point. . . . Yes, he had a conscience, and his conscience functioned in the expected way for about four weeks, whereupon it began to function the other way around."[1]

In Arendt's reconstruction, there were two keys to Eichmann's efficient execution of the official policy: first, his acceptance of the idea, particularly promoted by the S.S. head Heinrich Himmler, that mass killing represented a heroic task requiring great courage, loyalty to the Führer, and ability to bear the suffering involved in being an executioner; and, second, the "different personal attitude" (as Eichmann described it) he adopted as he became inured to seeing dead people all around him: "We did not care if we died today or only tomorrow."[2] Having redefined what is heroic (to accord with the prevailing view) and having become indifferent to human life, Eichmann was prepared to follow his new conscience. Although Arendt assumed that he had an "innate repugnance to crime," she did not raise any questions in her report about whether people generally are born with an instinct for evil or whether they are shaped early in their lives to a proclivity toward evil, whether radical or thoughtless. She explicitly stayed away from psychological inquiry—although when she returned fifteen years later to consider Eichmann in her last work, *The Life of the Mind,* she did employ a kind of philosophical psychology that encompassed his case.

What Arendt tried to capture with her phrase "the banality of evil" was the kind of evil that results from a particular capacity to stop thinking inherent in people like Eichmann, whose thoughtlessness was fostered by the fact that everyone around him went along unquestioningly with Hitler's extermination order and his vision of the glorious Thousand Year Reich. But her judgment had even greater resonance because she had been using this word, *thoughtless,* for years. When she was writing about life under modern conditions generally in her 1958 book *The Human Condition,* she had offered a definition of the term: "Thoughtlessness—the headless recklessness or hopeless confusion or complacent repetition of 'truths'" which have become trivial and empty—seems to me among the outstanding characteristics of our time."[3]

If the phrase "the banality of evil" is removed from the soundbite circuit, unpacked, explored, used as a catalyst for thought, held up as a lens, well then, it becomes more interesting, more challenging—it signifies a great deal. And if it is directed at Hannah Arendt's oeuvre, it will take you right to the core of her thinking, right to her abiding preoccupations, to the small cluster of hugely significant thoughts that she thought and rethought for all of her adult life. And it is because of these ideas and the example of how she used them that Arendt matters for us, now, as thinking and acting people, as citizens.

It was Arendt's opinion that a new type of criminal came into the world in the mid-twentieth century: the consequence-blind bureaucrat, agent of a criminal state, so unconcerned for the world— or alienated from it—that he could help lay waste to it, as it were, by the by. Rare courage and real thoughtfulness were needed to resist becoming caught up in the spread of such banal people and their thoughtlessly evil deeds across the whole surface of a society. As she wrote in her Eichmann report: "Under the conditions of the Third Reich, only 'exceptions' could be expected to react 'normally.' This simple truth of the matter created a dilemma for the [Israeli] judges which they could neither resolve nor escape."[4]

But Arendt did not believe that there was a type, certainly not a *new* type, of person who could resist the darkening slick of the banality of evil; rather, there were unique individuals whose actions were illuminating. "Even in the darkest times," she wrote in 1968, "we have a right to expect some illumination. [This] may well come less from theories and concepts than from the uncertain, flickering, and often weak light that some men and women, in their lives and works, will kindle under almost all circumstances and shed over the time given them on earth."[5]

"In dark times"—*in finsteren Zeiten*—was the poet Bertolt Brecht's formulation; there are evil deeds, even evil deeds of novel sorts, but they are not what constitute the darkness. The darkness is what comes when the open, light spaces between people, the public spaces where people can reveal themselves, are shunned or avoided; the darkness is a hateful attitude toward the public realm, toward politics. "History knows many periods of dark times in which the public realm has been obscured and the world become so dubious that people have ceased to ask any more of politics than that it show due consideration for their vital interests and personal liberty."[6] People who have given up on the world, thinking that they can set themselves outside it, without revealing themselves in the world or in the public realm, but only in private friendships or solitary pursuits, do not understand that "vital interests and personal liberty" pursued without heed for the rest of humankind become meaningless.

In her own life, Arendt had the good fortune to encounter and sometimes to befriend a number of remarkable illuminators. She held in special esteem her great teacher, the philosopher Karl Jaspers, a Protestant married to a Jewish woman who had stood firm and stated clearly in 1933 his opposition to the Nazis at a time when such a statement could easily have cost him his livelihood. He had stayed steady in his opposition throughout the next decade, living and teaching in Heidelberg, though that opposition could have cost him his life. Jaspers and his wife had been rescued in the last days of the Second World War just hours before they were scheduled for deportation to a concentration camp. After the war, Jaspers held an almost unique place among Arendt's acquaintances as an intellectual who never despised the world, never retreated into himself, but with a "sovereign naturalness"— a certain "cheerful recklessness"—exposed himself to the currents of public life, speaking out with consistent reasonableness on public issues.[7]

The contrast between Jaspers's experience in the period between 1933 and 1945 and that of Arendt's first important teacher, the philosopher Martin Heidegger at Marburg, her youthful love in the late 1920s, could not have been starker. Arendt had the traumatizing experience of watching this life-transforming professor become caught up—briefly, but not superficially—in the rising tide of National Socialism, for which he had foolishly imagined he could supply a philosophy. And then she had watched him retreat from the world into contemplative solitude and pour scorn upon the public realm, which he judged obfuscating, corrupting. Heidegger's "sarcastic, perverse-sounding statement, *Das Licht der Offentlichkeit verdunkelt alles* ('The light of the public obscures everything')" stood as an emblem for her of the attitude she considered the quintessence of irresponsibility toward the public world, which is, in her own view, the only place where truths people can share come to light.[8]

These two philosophers, Jaspers and Heidegger, each contributed crucial threads to the weave of experiences that turned Arendt from a student of philosophy into a political thinker. Their experiences and her experience of them can be found in everything she later wrote about politics, action, morality, friendship. Her own philosophizing always began from particular, concrete experience, which set her wondering, exploring.

As she became a writer after the war, Arendt refined her aim of discovering *basic* experiences, which she conceptualized and described in carefully chosen, illuminating detail. She specialized in analyzing people within their contexts, their historical moments, looking for what was new, without precedent, in their experience. Time and again, she would begin a sentence with "There have, of course, always been . . . " and conclude it with "but the truly novel feature is . . . " For example, a 1971 essay on the Pentagon Papers, "Lying in Politics," she discussed the presence throughout political history of lying and then focused specifically on the novel pervasiveness of lying in the Nazi regime. Arendt then turned to the present moment: "To the many genres in the art of lying developed in the past, we must now add two more recent varieties." One new genre was "the apparently innocuous one of the public-relations managers in government who learned their trade from the inventiveness of Madison Avenue." The other, more important, was a novel variety of lying, embraced by the extremely well-educated, theory-loving American government bureaucrats who conducted the Vietnam War: to deny or lie away facts that did not fit their theories; they made scientific-sounding assertions which they then tried to impose on reality, enacting their theories as if they were a script. These bureaucrats—these theoriocrats—hoped that reality would conform seamlessly to their lies, so that all their pseudoscientific theories about how the war was being won would be fulfilled, like magic.[9]

When she was identifying novelties, Arendt was working with her core idea that the era from after the First World War until the 1950s "thaw" in the Soviet Union represented a fundamental break in human history, a deep Before and After, that came about as fundamental assaults were made upon the very possibility of people gathering together to talk and act—of politics—assaults upon human plurality.[10] So, to understand who we are and what our human possibilities are in the After—by which Arendt meant not only after Nazism and Stalinism, or after the Second World War and the Holocaust, but after the advent of weapons with the capacity to destroy the human race—we have to think about what is *new* in these fundamental assaults upon the possibility of politics.

To think about what is new, we cannot use old concepts—particularly not concepts that have been emptied of their meaning and their usefulness by the very assaults that brought about this break in human history. We cannot use concepts from Before, inherited from a world that exists no longer, to explore the After. But it is not possible simply to set aside old concepts—like old hats that we can remove from our heads—without exploring the fact that those concepts are inside our heads, ingrained in our thinking. Because habits of thinking linger, we also have to change our habits by understanding how they have been acquired. Both as a thinker and as a critic, an explorer of the conditions and habits of thinking, Hannah Arendt was exemplary, especially because these two activities were never separate for her.

It was her standard procedure to single out a concept and start asking how humans, through their entire recorded history (or at least that part of it recorded in European languages she could read), had used that concept to present their experiences. She would identify shifts in experience by applying her strongly imaginative philological divining rod to the key conceptual word. What is politics? What is freedom? What is authority? Finally, her question would become: In our unprecedented era, what shifts in word use have come about or are coming about or need to come about? Have our words caught up to our new experiences? Sometimes she would invent a new word or define a word in a new way to point to an experience that she had determined was new. "The banality of evil," to go back to that, was meant to reveal a new kind of criminal and a new kind of crime.

In the early 1950s, Arendt had proposed the then unfamiliar word *totalitarianism* (first coined by Mussolini in the 1920s) for a form of government that she judged to be new and not comparable to the other, well-known forms with their names as old as the Greeks: monarchy, aristocracy, oligarchy, democracy. The government of Nazi Germany was totalitarian, and so, she argued, was Stalin's Soviet Union. After she published *The Origins of Totalitarianism* in 1951, her analysis and her new word, *totalitarianism*, had quite a career (which it will be important to examine later); now, more than fifty years later, as much of its original illumination has been obscured, *totalitarianism*, too, has become a sound bite, a cliché, for many who use it, while for some it has become integral to the scientific-sounding theories that guide their foreign policy decisions.

A new concept must continually be squared with new realities, or it, too, can become a constraint on thinking. Arendt wanted thoughts and words adequate to the new world and able to dissolve clichés, reject thoughtlessly received ideas, break down hackneyed analyses, expose lies and bureaucratic doubletalk, help people withdraw from their addiction to propagandistic images. Usually it is poets or poetic thinkers who live by an expectation that language will deliver us from the temptation not to think; they take responsibility for telling the story of what really happened, displaying "the inner truth of the event."[11] Hannah Arendt was that rare being: a thinker of poetic capacity and devotion who was not a poet but was, rather, an analyst, a practical-minded person who used distinction making to break things down into their component parts and show how they worked.

In the years since Arendt's death, it seems to me, this emphasis of hers on identifying what is unprecedented has become less and less appreciated. Even while she was alive, the prevailing tendency among intellectuals was to look for historical analogies to current events, and this habit has grown even stronger in recent years. Most intellectuals suggest that there are "lessons of the past" from which we can learn, or that those who remember the past will not be condemned to repeat it (thereby underestimating how crucial it is not just to remember the past but to think about it, show its meaning, so as to avoid being caught up in the *compulsion* to repeat that is typical of those haunted by raw memory). Hoping to ensure that the world would "never again!" suffer the horrors totalitarian regimes had inflicted on their external enemies and on their own people, intellectuals in the free world, for example, zeroed in on the word *appeasement*. Every decision not to go to war or any decision to pursue diplomacy in the face of provocation became appeasement, similar to the caving in of British prime minister Neville Chamberlain to Hitler's demands in 1938. In the early 1960s successive American governments, disastrously subscribing to a scientific-sounding theory called "the domino theory," said that America must not appease the Soviet Union or China or the lead domino (North Vietnam) waiting to fall onto South Vietnam and make the whole of Asia a bastion of communism.

The habit of thinking—or not thinking, being thoughtless—in historical analogies and precedents became so strong in the postwar era that when the World Trade Center was attacked by terrorists in 2001, the "Attack on America" was immediately analogized to Pearl Harbor. In a flash, the American people were encouraged to assume that the American response should be war, as though al-Qaeda were a nation-state like Japan, connected to an Axis (this time the "Axis of Evil," which itself became the target when Iraq was invaded in 2003). Right away, Osama bin Laden was Hitler. Soon after, Saddam Hussein was a totalitarian.

It seems to me that Hannah Arendt, had she been alive in 2001, would have gone straight to her writing table to protest that the World Trade Center was not Pearl Harbor and that "war on terror" was a meaningless phrase. Terror is not an enemy, it is a method, a means. I can imagine her bringing to bear an argument that she made in both *On Revolution* and *On Violence:* to the right and to the left of the political spectrum, among people who have dedicated their lives to preventing revolution and among those who have put their hopes in it, violence has become so habitual and easily rationalized that politicians, revolutionaries, and now terrorists no longer even wonder whether the violence they want to undertake might do more harm than good, especially in cases where there is no identified, or even identifiable, enemy. Violence is what it takes to "make history." Arendt drew distinctions (which we shall consider later) between acting and making and between violence and power, which were not well understood in 2001 and which still are not well understood, but which are, to my mind, distinctions without which we—the people—cannot understand our world. And we are in terrible peril because of our ignorance.

To agree with that assessment, you have to share my opinion that making distinctions and conceptualizing matter; that how we, as a people, think about what we are doing matters. And we need a "how to" example of thinking that matters. Whenever I imagine to myself how Hannah Arendt—who was my teacher— might have judged some phenomenon and brought clarity to it for others, I hear her heavily German-accented voice carefully saying: "Vell, vell, on one hand . . . und den on another hand . . . Und, look here, consider it this way . . . " Then she pauses, and you can actually see in her face how much she is mentally enjoying what Kant referred to as the "enlarged mentality" of opinion sharing, consulting, paying calls on other points of view: "*Aber sehen Sie mal!* [But look sharp!] Here is the other side, another perspective." There were never *any* sound bites.

No, that's not entirely right. I do remember an evening, after she had sat listening and shaking her head as a well-known American intellectual gave a lecture. The judgment she rendered could *qualify* as a sound bite, even though it came from an unlikely source—a footnote in *The Critique of Pure Reason,* by her dear old thinking-companion Immanuel Kant: "For stupidity, there is no cure."[12]

Recently, as our world has grown darker, as America—the nation Arendt admired before all others, her home after twelve years of being a stateless refugee—has grown further and further removed from its founding principles, which all concerned respect for the public realm, I have frequently found myself wondering: What would Arendt have said? What would she think of this world we live in, three decades after her death? What would she consider importantly *new* about it?

In this book I wish to show how Arendt thought and how she arrived at the judgments she made about her era, the era of totalitarianisms and their sequels, which she called "the modern world." I want to address myself particularly to younger readers, students of the age I was when I became Arendt's student in 1968, and she became for me and my fellow students what Jaspers had been for her, a light in dark times.

There will be biographical strands in this book, but it is not an abbreviation of the biography I published in 1982, *Hannah Arendt: For Love of the World.* I think of what I am doing now as a conversation with her, a continuation into the present of the conversation I have been having with her in my mind since 1968. It is now 2006, the centenary of Arendt's birth, and all over the world people are preparing to celebrate the event with conferences, photo and art exhibitions, publications, a Web site (www .hannaharendt.org) sponsored by the two Hannah Arendt Centers, and even the official opening of Hannah Arendt Strasse, a small street near the Holocaust Memorial in Berlin, a stone's throw from the old Brandenburg Gate, which was reduced to rubble by Allied bombs in 1945 but is now reconstructed. So this is an especially good time to revisit her thinking, to put to her imaginatively the questions that come to mind when reading the morning paper or receiving the pulse of events by the kinds of electronic technologies that she could only glimpse in their in-fancies, at the beginning of the global village.

Neither I, her biographer, nor anyone else should presume to *know* what Hannah Arendt would have thought about any event, trend, idea, person, or group that she did not look upon with her own fiercely observant eyes and the eyes of her uniquely and inim-itably brilliant mind. Here, I am only going to *wonder* about what she might have thought, and do so by engaging—wondering about—how and what she did think, as evidenced by her writing and conversations

To wonder, Aristotle wrote—and Arendt loved to cite him, rolling out the Greek word for *wonder, thaumadzein*—is to begin to philosophize. It is to stop and think; to pause and reflect; to allow yourself the alertness to be struck, surprised, and to respond without too much presupposition or prejudgment. This is intended to be a journey of wonder, but I shall begin it more prosaically by reviewing how Arendt's reputation has developed in the years since her death, placing the full scope of the publications I am going to draw upon for my wondering before you to keep in mind.

In the three decades since her death, Hannah Arendt has become *the* analyst—of totalitarian regimes, of revolutionary types, of forms of violence and war—for theorists and activists who consider the contemporary situations of citizens, nations, and international relations. Her vision of the possibilities for freedom in political life has currency around the world. But how did she become a figure of such historical importance? Let me begin by mapping the territory of her posthumous publications, which has grown with her influence and which is increasing that influence and illuminating it. Since the appearance in 1978 of *The Life of the Mind,* the last third of which was left only in notes, an extensive shelf of her writings has been published. There are writings of three sorts: correspondence; collections of unpublished or uncollected German and English essays; and a *Denktagebuch,* an intellectual diary, issued in 2003 in Germany, where it sold out its first edition despite its 1,500-page length and 120-euro price tag.

There are now three (and will eventually be five) volumes of the essays, all published under the thoughtful and erudite editorship of Jerome Kohn, who was also her last research assistant during the years when we were both her students. *Essays in Understanding* appeared in 1994. *Responsibility and Judgment,* incorporating a long text on moral philosophy that Kohn crafted out of rough lecture manuscripts, appeared in 2003. *The Promise of Politics,* containing a book-length manuscript on Marx and several other important lectures, came out in 2005. The final volumes will consist of a collection of Arendt's Jewish writings and a volume containing short essays culled from the Denktagebuch.

Within the next few years, a *Selected Letters* will also appear, and the full range of Arendt's letter-writing activity will be available (although it can be accessed completely now at the New School for Social Research and at the Hannah Arendt Center in Germany via a digitized version of the Library of Congress Arendt Papers). Of the already published correspondence, the one with Karl Jaspers, appearing in German in 1985 and in English in 1992, has already joined the ranks of the twentieth-century classics in the genre. All future historians of the European American world will turn to it for its detailed, in-depth—and remarkably prescient—reflections on the "crises of the republic" in postwar America and on Germany's political recovery and struggle toward "mastery of the past" after the Nazis.

Within Four Walls (2000), the letters exchanged over the thirty-five years of their partnership by Arendt and Heinrich Blücher,

her working-class Berlin-born self-educated, intellectually charismatic husband, offer a loving conversation, sustained throughout the exigencies of emigration, acculturation, professional struggles, illness, loss, and wonder at the New World. Some sense of Blücher's philosophical projects—he was a teacher at Bard College but not a writer—can be gleaned from the correspondence, particularly his abiding reverence for Socrates (who was also a teacher but not a writer) and his devotion to Karl Jaspers's vision of a cosmopolitan philosophy. Jaspers had imagined a colloquy with philosophers from all the parts of the world that trace their cultural histories to the Axial Age (600–300 BCE); and he had set down this colloquy in *The Great Philosophers*, grouping the philosophers according to their thinking styles and their shared questions and themes. Not a chronological handing down of ideas but a "spiritual juxtaposition" orders his study.

This vision of a global philosophical conversation spanning the ages, which both Blücher and Arendt shared with Jaspers, will be key to my exploration of how Arendt would have looked upon our globalizing world. But what the correspondence itself shows most vividly is how Arendt and Blücher provided each other with the safe "four walls" of their home and their conversation, where each could depend upon the other's loyalty and deep honesty about their strengths and weaknesses, their shared hopes; where plurality and equality were assured. It could be said about Arendt's marriage to Blücher what she said about the marriage of Karl and Gertrude Jaspers: "From this world in miniature, he has learned, as from a model, what is essential in the whole realm of human affairs."[13]

Arendt's friendship with Mary McCarthy is chronicled in a witty, often acerbic, and delightfully gossipy exchange of political and cultural commentary. *Between Friends* (1995) is the most American of Arendt's volumes of correspondence, the one that will be crucial reading for students of American twentieth-century literary life, while her exchanges with the major but still little-known novelist Hermann Broch and the Zionist leader Kurt Blumenfeld will probably not soon be translated into English or find audiences beyond professional German scholars.

Between Friends illuminates the way the friendship between Arendt and McCarthy grew and what its nature was. Arendt always had a *beste Freundin*, though McCarthy was the first American woman for whom she felt an affinity. McCarthy was six years younger, but she had the qualities that Arendt needed in friends and had found in her husband to an extraordinary degree: a passion for observing and judging the world—both their immediate social world and the larger political world—emotionality and "heart" without sentimentality; intelligence without cant, self-indulgent cleverness, or subservience to the opinions of others; loyalty and an understanding of how friendships make a home for those without traditional family, community, or religious settings.

Arendt could also depend upon McCarthy for a vicarious experience of the complex involvements with men she herself had had in her youth (and told McCarthy about) but did not have or want to have in the thirty-five years of her marriage and dedication to writing. She could be McCarthy's confidante—almost the Jewish mother, certainly the older sister—experiencing Mc-

Carthy's imbroglios often without leaving her writing desk. She could let McCarthy take the path she had rejected of novel writing, celebrity, literary salon life, and political activism, and receive in turn entrée into that world: an infusion of vivacity and literary society and intellectual insight. In her correspondence with McCarthy, Arendt felt free to reveal her moods—the times when she was depressed or discouraged—and to show how much she wanted and needed to be a woman, a friend, not a famous person or a person whose intellectual work was on a higher plane than that of anyone around her. And McCarthy was European enough, as a traveler and as a writer, to appreciate Arendt as politically American but culturally and in sensibility always a European cosmopolitan. In the years after Blücher's death in 1970, when Jaspers, too, was gone, McCarthy understood her friend's mourning and provided her with the repose of those "four walls."

The letters—available in German in 1999, then in English in 2004—that Arendt exchanged between 1925 and 1975 with Martin Heidegger differ from the other published correspondence in a number of ways. These letters were closed in the Marbach Literary Archive soon after Heidegger's death in 1976, only months after Arendt's. Unlike the other collections of correspondence, the one with Heidegger is incomplete. Most of Heidegger's letters are included in the published edition, but relatively few of Arendt's survived. Her letters from the beginning of their affair in Marburg (1925–1927), when Heidegger was writing his masterwork, *Sein und Zeit,* are missing, so her initial experience of the relationship cannot be read in her own words. When they met again in 1950, while Heidegger was still under a teaching ban because of his Nazi Party membership and his reprehensible pro-Hitler actions as rector of Freiberg University, he wrote to her voluminously, but only a few of her letters to him survived. Only after 1967 is there a real correspondence to be read. The thorough and meticulous editor of the correspondence, Ursula Ludz, supplies a book within a book of notes, many referring to Arendt's writings and correspondence with Jaspers and Blücher about Heidegger, who never wrote a public word about Arendt.

The second thing that distinguishes this correspondence is that its publication was preceded by a scandal. The scandal was created—quite intentionally—by a professor at MIT named Elżbieta Ettinger, who managed to obtain permission to read the unpublished Arendt-Heidegger letters and quote from Arendt's side only in a short dual biography.[14] When her book appeared in 1995, the fact that Arendt and Heidegger had been lovers in the 1920s was public knowledge because I had revealed it in my biography. My version, which triggered no scandal, was based on interviews with those few of Arendt's friends who knew about it and the few references to it in Arendt's letters, especially to her husband.

Ettinger's version, although drawing on the Arendt-Heidegger letters, is a fantasy—or what Arendt in her 1971 essay on the Pentagon Papers called "an image," bearing little relation to reality. Ettinger projected a naive and helpless Jewish schoolgirl and a charming but ruthless married Catholic professor playing out a drama of passionate recklessness and betrayal, followed by slavish loyalty on the part of the betrayed mistress. Ettinger's Hannah Arendt is never able to grow beyond the romance; she masochistically stands by her man with "unquestioning loyalty." Keeping her youthful affair secret from her husband for fifteen years, she blames all Heidegger's shortcomings on his wife and exercises scandalously poor judgment both as his apologist ("she did what she could to whitewash his Nazi past") and as the "ambassador of good will" he wanted her to be ("Arendt accepted the assignment"). This is Ettinger's judgment on Arendt's motivation: "She exculpated him not as much out of loyalty, compassion, or a sense of justice as out of her own need to save her pride and dignity."[15] That is, Arendt had to make Heidegger into a man she could respect in order to respect herself.

Ettinger's work is spiked with hundreds of qualifiers—"it appears," "one can imagine," "she must have felt"—yet presents these dubious statements as though they were facts, the sign of a biographer trapped inside her *own* story and drawing her subject into the trap with her. There is none of the dialogue with the subject that infused the character study Arendt herself produced in *Men in Dark Times.* So it is not surprising that this fantasy caused glee in the camps of Arendt's enemies, of whom she had not a few, and distress to her supporters, who could not at that time access the correspondence for themselves.

The third thing that distinguishes this correspondence from the others is that Heidegger was not—like Jaspers, Blücher, McCarthy, Broch, or Blumenfeld—a person who could share Arendt's unrelenting interest in the affairs of the world, which developed after their affair and, in part, in reaction to it, as a cure for her own youthful unworldliness. (The *cura posterior* began when she left Heidegger to study with Jaspers, to whom she later marveled,

"How well your philosophy prepared me for politics.")[16] Heidegger was not, as the other correspondents were, someone who took responsibility and exercised—relished exercising—judgment. Among the Germans, he was the great philosopher of the twentieth century, while Jaspers was the great political philosopher, but he was not an exemplary mensch.

As is clear in her letters to Jaspers and Blücher, Arendt was shocked and pained by Heidegger's duplicity, his divided self; his character was frequently a topic of her private and public writings, although she did not write an extended study of him in the manner she reserved for those she admired. Arendt never finished working on the puzzle of Martin Heidegger, and at the time of her death she was still writing about him in *The Life of the Mind*, where she drew on the reading of his work she had offered him in an eightieth-birthday tribute (included in the *Letters*) and clearly rejected his philosophy.

Among the many commentators who have made a controversy out of the Arendt-Heidegger relationship, shaping the posthumous reputations of both, there are basically two positions. In one, Heidegger is first and foremost a member of the Nazi Party who never publicly recanted his decision to join or his actions as a party member. Arendt, from this perspective, was an apologist for Heidegger because she renewed their relationship after the war and worked to have Heidegger's writings translated into English. In the second position, Heidegger is first and foremost a great philosopher whose lapse in judgment and actions can be understood as analogous to Plato's journey to Syracuse to try to make a philosopher-king out of the tyrant Dionysus. From this perspective, Arendt's respect for Heidegger's philosophy and her indebtedness to it in her own work are understandable, and the key question is whether philosophers have ever had anything of value to offer political actors or whether their activity will (or should) always be of another world—the contemplative world.

Arendt's own judgment about Heidegger, which was different from both of these positions, evolved over the postwar years. Before 1950, when she was writing *The Origins of Totalitarianism,* she angrily viewed him as a typical European philistine who had been attracted to "the mob" but had found no place ultimately in the party of the mob, which had no interest in creative individuals like him. In 1946 she included him in a list of outstanding German scholars who "did their utmost to supply the Nazis with ideas and techniques." Later, when she renewed her relationship with him, she tried to explain him psychologically as a divided character, part genuine, part mendacious or cowardly and dependent on the appreciation of (at worst) sycophants and (at best) people who were not on his intellectual level. She and Jaspers argued about whether Heidegger could overcome his inner division; Arendt argued for patience while Jaspers chose to break off his friendship with Heidegger. [17]

Finally, in the 1960s, Arendt came to understand Heidegger differently, on the basis of a thorough study of his wartime work as well as their conversations. She then emphasized that in the late 1930s he had written into the second volume of his *Nietzsche* not a political recantation of his Nazi Party membership but at least a philosophical statement about "the will not to will." Having given up his foolish hope of influencing the Nazi leadership, he renounced both willing and the world where willing people gather for action and retired to his "residence of thinking." With that "turn" (*Kehre*), he wrote about the will in a manner that she later summarized in *The Life of the Mind*: "In Heidegger's understanding, the will to rule and dominate is a kind of original sin, of which he found himself guilty when he tried to come to terms with his brief past in the Nazi movement."[18] In private, his repentance led to her forgiveness, but Arendt was very clear about the difference between forgiving a person and forgiving his actions.

The development of Arendt's judgment of Heidegger is not well known, particularly because *The Life of the Mind* remains her least-read and least-understood book, among both political theorists and historians and American and European philosophers, who have not yet accorded her the attention that the philosophical writings of her last years deserve. But the controversy that has arisen over the Arendt-Heidegger relationship has contributed significantly to the kind of historical figure Arendt has become. Even when she is revered, questions about her judgment shadow her. This is even more the case with the other controversy that has continued after her death to shape her reception in the world of ideas—the one that began after the Eichmann trial and became so well known in Europe that it was spoken of simply as the Controversy, *Die Kontroverse*.

Interestingly, the various positions taken in the 1960s by participants in the Controversy are still being taken, and almost everyone fights with an image of the book, not with what it actually says. Fear of anti-Semitism in its old and its ever new forms as well as fixed ideas about how to combat anti-Semitism fuel the repetition compulsion in the Controversy. This rigidity has had the unfortunate result that the most immediately relevant practical dimension of *Eichmann in Jerusalem*, Arendt's concluding reflection on the challenge his trial made to international law, has hardly been heard—even now, when an international court has been formed in The Hague to try those who commit "crimes against humanity" as the agents of criminal states. She noted: "The court [in Jerusalem] was confronted with a crime it could not find in the lawbooks and with a criminal whose like was unknown in any court, at least prior to the Nuremberg Trials."[19] During Arendt's lifetime, the law books still ignored "crimes against humanity"; they did not even supply an adequate definition of the term despite what was learned in Jerusalem.

Both these controversies over Arendt's judgment call into question the way in which she thought about judging, which was to have been the topic of the third, unfinished segment of *The Life of the Mind*. I shall return to the topic of judgment when I consider *The Life of the Mind* later, but I want to remark here that having all Arendt's correspondence fully available over the past two decades has brought me an understanding of her way of thinking and judging that I did not have earlier—or had only indistinctly.

In my biography, I stressed how important to Arendt were her husband, who was her friend, and her tribe of other friends, especially Jaspers as a European and McCarthy as an American. But I can see now that she appreciated deeply what *Freundschaft* can offer to thinking and judging even when she was in her twenties and still a philosophy student without political experience. She began work in the late 1920s on a biography of the eighteenth-century salon hostess Rahel Varnhagen, and it is clear (and clearer now that her letters are available) how in this book she was trying both to understand retrospectively her relationship with Heidegger and to distinguish herself from him and the unworldly quality of his philosophy, its uncommunicativeness. In her biography, she explored Varnhagen's way of living and thinking, focusing on her unsuccessful search for a person—a friend—who would love her and accept her while she struggled to love and accept herself. As much as she felt a kinship with Varnhagen, Arendt did not want to repeat her subject's mistakes a century and a half later or fail in her own search for friendship and for what she would later call "political friendship," or sometimes simply "respect," a bond with others who also desired to share a world even if they had differing opinions about how to do so.

Arendt presented Varnhagen as a refreshingly naive woman, without the prejudices of the privileged and self-regarding celebrities around her, who had what she did not: cultivation, wealth, beauty, and freedom from the stigma of having been born Jewish (a stigmatization Arendt herself was fortunate not to feel). No habit of speculation or received ideas obscured the world for Varnhagen. She "was compelled to grasp everything for herself as if encountering it for the first time. . . . From this freedom was derived her striking manner of describing things, people and situations. Her wit, which had made her redoubtable even as a young girl, was merely her completely untrammeled manner of looking at things."[20]

But Arendt's biography is a story of how those whom Varnhagen hoped would be her friends and reassure her about her reality as a person failed her, and of how she failed herself, too. Varnhagen and the men with whom she had relationships shared the key failing of the Romantics, what Arendt calls "escape from self," meaning self-in-relation-to-others. They all tried in their individual ways to make themselves into a unique work of art. For them, "thinking amounted to an enlightened kind of magic which could substitute for, evoke and predict experience, the world and society." The Romantics escaped from a true, related self into an inauthentic, unrealistic self, unable to face the future because they were lost in introspection and unable to see the past because they were lost in sentimentality. "Thus the power and autonomy of the soul are secured. Secured at the price of truth, it must be recognized, for *without reality shared with other human beings, truth loses all meaning*" (emphasis mine).[21]

Remarkably, at twenty-five Hannah Arendt was able to reach this conclusion, which guided her whole life. And as she found true friends, she managed to avoid making the Romantic mistake. But she continued to encounter it in others. In one of her postwar ruminations on Heidegger, Arendt identified him as "the last (one hopes) Romantic,"[22] but it is clear in her correspondence with the others who did give her the "reality shared with other human beings" that she had discovered why Romanticism had not ended with Heidegger. In the decades after the war, it changed form and became politically even more dangerous. She then called escape from self "world-alienation," and identified it as rebellion against "the human condition." In her last years, Arendt observed the magical thinkers who wanted to make a work of art of themselves so ardently that they even tried to manipulate reality so that it confirmed them—conformed *to them*—as the people they wanted to be. She encountered world-alienated self-image manufacturing celebrated with what we now call "spin." The term *Romantic* is not often revived for such celebrities—the psychological term *narcissist* is more common. But her critique of those to whom it applies retains its nearly seventy-five-year-long truth.

one

*The Origins of
Totalitarianism*
and the Twenty-
first Century

Even as a young biographer Arendt recognized that if you wanted to understand *what* a person thought you also had to understand *how* that person thought. Furthermore, if you wanted to understand whether that thought stayed close to the realities of the world, you had to understand how the person behaved in communicative relationships, that is, relationships "concerned with the common world, which remains 'inhuman' in a very literal sense unless it is constantly talked about by human beings."[1]

When Arendt began writing *The Origins of Totalitarianism* (published in 1951), after a decade of life as a refugee, the conditions that would enable her to face reality—conditions that she had only envisioned in the Varnhagen biography—were in place. *The Origins of Totalitarianism* is the work of a woman who has grown into her insights. In this work Heinrich Blücher anchored her; in addition he brought his passion and perspective as a self-taught military historian to his wife's book, a fact she acknowledged by dedicating it to him. Arendt was also in constant correspondence with Karl Jaspers, visiting him yearly. In her steadied, fierce engagement with the world, she had produced a book that no Romantic, past or present, could have imagined.

Reading *The Origins of Totalitarianism* is like visiting a museum where there is a giant mural of the nineteenth and twentieth centuries that you can never finish taking in—a vast historians' *Guernica*. It has richer insights on the topics it engages than shelves of other volumes; even its footnotes contain more ideas than many books. I remember vividly my first sustained encounter with it, during a New School seminar with Hans Morgenthau, the author of a book called *Politics Among Nations* that had, when it appeared in 1948, defined the field of international relations scholarship and delineated a position called "political realism." Arendt had told me to take his seminar, explaining, "It will be very practical for you." She viewed her old friend and fellow émigré as a practical man—that is, a man of praxis, action. And the action for which she and all us students considered him a hero was his resignation from the National Security Council—he was the only member of Lyndon Johnson's administration to take such a step—in protest over the Vietnam War, which he had started to criticize publicly in 1965.[2] This was an exemplary action, a light in dark times.

The man of action's syllabus for a course on twentieth-century politics was made up of works like *The Origins of Totalitarianism* that he used as lenses, very much in Arendt's manner. If you observe the world through the lens of this book, what do you see? Morgenthau shared with Arendt a disdain—almost a contempt—for the way politics was studied in American universities, and he offered these books, Arendt's in particular, as models of how political theory should be written. "You can fight over many things with her," her told us in his heavy accent; "but she was the first to *understand* fascism. Then all the professors came along years later to make details where she was the pioneer. She was a historian very close up, like Thucydides."

By "the first to *understand* fascism," Morgenthau meant that Arendt had drawn up a field manual on the subject. No one reading *The Origins of Totalitarianism* carefully would ever again have trouble identifying a regime as fascist (or, as she preferred to say, protototalitarian). As he discussed Arendt's book with us, Morgenthau had one key question for it: Was the American state at the end of the 1960s becoming fascist? His answer, backed by her field manual, was that though there were many fascistic or protototalitarian elements in America, and much danger, the protections American democracy still afforded were keeping the country from descending into totalitarianism.

Morgenthau's question—Was America becoming fascist?—was a variation on the question Arendt herself had in mind as she composed *The Origins of Totalitarianism:* Would it be possible, by understanding totalitarianism, to judge future totalitarianisms accurately as they arose or in their infancy? She was searching for criteria by which to judge such states. To see how she arrived at her criteria—how she wrote her field manual—we must first step back and look at the composition and reception of *The Origins of Totalitarianism.*

Published in America in 1951, when its author was forty-five years old, *The Origins of Totalitarianism* passed through more versions than any of her many other books. A biography of the book, encompassing its gestation, its birth, its development, and the reactions to it (which continue to the present day), would illuminate how the political history of the first half of the twentieth century was understood in the second half. That story is being retold every day at the opening of our new century. You can hear it when American politicians refer—for example—to the "United Islamic Front" desired by Osama bin Laden as a kind of imperialism or a kind of totalitarianism. The present U.S. secretary of state, Condoleezza Rice, a Sovietologist, refers as frequently to the threat of totalitarianism as did President Ronald Reagan with his 1950s-style rhetoric about the "Evil Empire."

During the years from 1941 to 1949 Arendt envisaged, reframed, reorganized, and expanded *The Origins of Totalitarianism* many times, reacting to new realities as they became clear to her. Her first vision of the book had come soon after she wrote a series of articles in 1941 for the German-language New York newspaper *Aufbau,* advocating a Jewish army as part of the Allied military effort. Her initial plan was to show how the Jews had come into the storm center of European politics and to point a way for them to think and act politically in response to their position. She began reading widely to try to set modern anti-Semitism in the context of European imperialism, both at home and abroad. Her argument was that modern anti-Semitism, promulgated by political parties and fueled by racism, was fundamentally different from religious anti-Semitism—that *political* anti-Semitism was novel.

In the winter of 1942–1943, however, she was propelled to a starker, deeper vision. As news of the Nazi concentration camps reached America, her book became her way to respond not as a historian, concerned with the past and its causality, but as a political thinker to the unbelievable fact that killing factories were operating day and night all over Nazi-controlled Eastern Europe. Twenty years later, she looked back on the moment in an interview, using the plural to emphasize that she was sharing her assessment with Blücher and their émigré group: "At first [early in 1943] we did not believe it . . . because it was militarily unnecessary and uncalled for. . . . A half a year later, when it was proven to us, we finally believed it. Before that, one would say to oneself—so, we all have enemies. That's quite natural. Why should a people have no enemies? But this was different. This was as though the abyss had opened. Because one always had the hope that everything else might someday be rectified, politically—that everything might be put right again. This couldn't be. This should never have been allowed to happen. . . . None of us could reconcile ourselves to it."[3]

As she read memoirs of survivors and documents from the postwar Nuremburg Trials, Arendt interpreted the concentration camps as a key development in what she had been calling "race imperialism." She began to develop this idea in a manuscript entitled "The Elements of Shame: Antisemitism—Imperialism—Racism." Building on the interpretation, she shifted the book's trajectory toward the shame of the camps, in which, for no *political* purpose, people were dominated, terrorized, deprived of their rights and their "right to have rights," of their capacity to act, and finally of their now completely devalued lives. She focused on torture, a focus from which we can learn a great deal these days, when torture is—alarmingly—being justified by American government officials as a legitimate means to allegedly political ends.

Eventually, Arendt collected everything she had written between 1943 and 1946 into the first two parts ("Antisemitism" and "Imperialism") of the book she retitled *The Origins of Totalitarianism* and then composed a new third part that she called "Totalitarianism." This final section argued that the concentration camps were the defining institution of an unprecedented form of government that was neither a deformation of tyranny nor an extreme of authoritarian dictatorship. In a totalitarian state, not a single leader but a party that has abolished all other parties establishes absolute power in the wake of a political movement that has broken down all social and class formations and created a "mass society." This new form of government, without political opposition or traditional forms of community to check it, reaches into every facet of life with institutions of total terror, among them secret police and, especially, concentration camps. Arendt was able to delineate this form of government in general terms by discovering a comparable particular. Through materials from the Soviet Union that were beginning to become available in the West—including an anonymous memoir titled *The Dark Side of the Moon*—Arendt had grasped that the Stalinist regime, too, as defined by its institutions of total terror—the KGB, the purges, the labor camps—was totalitarian. "The really essential things—which I have to put together with Russia," she wrote to Jaspers in September 1947, "are just now coming clear to me."[4] Her analysis developed from existing facts; it was not preformed.

While she was finishing *The Origins of Totalitarianism,* an anti-Communist movement, capitalized on by Senator Joseph McCarthy, had begun to gather momentum in America. Coloring the third part of *The Origins of Totalitarianism* and a number of essays written in the years before and just after its publication, the McCarthy phenomenon intensified Arendt's search for a new understanding of totalitarianism. She articulated her essential thought as a call to action that needed to be guided by "a new political principle . . . a new law on earth."[5] Politics—in the sense of citizens speaking and acting in public, variously allowed by different forms of government and secured by their laws—appears only under certain historical conditions. By the same token, politics can also disappear. Totalitarianism, she argued, is the disappearance of politics: a form of government that destroys politics, methodically eliminating speaking and acting human beings and attacking the very humanity of first a selected group and then all groups. In this way, totalitarianism makes people superfluous as human beings. This is its radical evil.

In diverse ways, this essential thought of Arendt's was picked up by reviews and discussions that greeted her book in 1951 in America and Europe. But most of her respondents were trapped in the preformed ways of thinking she had struggled to transcend. They were impervious to her urgent message: "An insight into the nature of totalitarian rule, directed by our fear of the concentration camp, might serve to devaluate all outmoded political shadings from left to right, and, beside and above them, to introduce the most essential political criterion for judging the events of our time: will it lead to totalitarian rule or will it not?"[6]

On the American and European right, Arendt's analysis was welcomed because it could be interpreted as implying that to be anti-Communist was to be antitotalitarian. Opposing not just the Soviet Union but also Marxist ideology took on the moral rightness of opposing Nazi Germany and Nazi ideology. Arendt realized soon after the publication of her book that the mainstays of McCarthyite anticommunism in America were former Communists. The rigid intellectual mode of this group was, in its new allegiance, unchanged. In terms of their fundamental disposition of character and thought, the anti-Communists were ideologues who could change causes without dislocation and whose dictate was, simply, that the end justifies the means. Victory for democracy over totalitarianism, they held, justified any means for promoting democracy—including totalitarian means.

On the American and European left, Communists and socialists objected to two aspects of Arendt's theory: her disregard of their belief that a fascist regime is the opposite of a Marxist revolutionary government and her neglect of their argument that the Soviet Union under Stalin was a betrayal of Marxism and Marxism's concern with social justice. This critical perspective made it virtually impossible for readers on the left to appreciate Arendt's attention to the *elements* of totalitarianism and the antipolitical processes by which these elements had crystallized and might again crystallize into totalitarianism. The belief that Arendt was a voice of the American Cold War was particularly intense in France, where, in 1951 anti-Americanism was widespread (fueled by fear of the Marshall Plan as an assault on French sovereignty). Although often cited in French political debates, *The Origins of Totalitarianism* was not translated into French for almost twenty years. Only when the French intellectual climate had been changed by the generation of 1968 did scholarship on Arendt begin to proliferate, preparing the way for a recent French edition of *Origins* containing its many prefaces and additions.

The reception of Arendt's book in Germany was especially complex, in part because the Nazi past remained, in the familiar phrase, "unmastered." In addition, Arendt's commitment to a "comity of nations"—by which she meant a federation of European states—challenged unreconstructed German nationalists of all kinds, as it still does in the face of the European Union's aspiration to federalism. Initially, however, her work was enthusiastically received by a small group around the journal *Die Wandlung,* of which Jaspers was an editor. As a genuinely European rather than simply German journal, *Die Wandlung* was closer to being beyond all outmoded political shadings from left to right than any publication then being produced in Europe.

On Arendt's first return to Germany, in the winter of 1949–1950, she met up again with Jaspers, and they began thinking more concretely about what a comity of nations might look like. Meanwhile, her impressions of Germany were recorded in an article called "The Aftermath of Nazi Rule," published in the new Jewish magazine *Commentary*—an article that can be read as an addendum to *The Origins of Totalitarianism.*[7] Nazism had been worse than a tyranny for the Germans, she noted, because totalitarianism "kills the roots" of a people's political, social, and personal life. It was 1952 before she expressed any optimism that the roots of the German people might ever regenerate. In that year German voters made what she saw as a halting start at repudiating the Nazi past. Abandoning what she called their "primitive nationalism," they committed themselves to a vision of a future Europe, represented by Konrad Adenauer's support for the proposed European Defense Community (EDC). But Arendt soon came to distrust both the vote and Adenauer himself, whose advocacy of a "Christian Europe" and restoration of the national army she viewed as re-Nazification. When she finally found a German publisher for *Origins* and translated it into her native language in 1953, she dejectedly expected her views on Nazi and Soviet totalitarianism to be distorted and exploited by the Adenauer majority, just as they were by the American anti-Communists. She was right.

Arendt revised and updated *Origins* once more for a 1958 edition, which concluded with a new essay called "Ideology and Terror" in which she justified in more detail her claim that Stalin's Soviet Union had been totalitarian. In an epilogue focused on the 1956 Hungarian Revolution, she explored developments in the Soviet Union after Stalin and praised an institution that arose spontaneously in Hungary and was diametrically opposed to the logic that led to concentration or labor camps: the revolutionary councils.

While she was making these revisions, Arendt became aware that among many social scientists her careful distinctions about aspects of totalitarianism were little appreciated and that even the goal of making distinctions was rarely valued. So in several essays she marched forward to scold: "There exists . . . a silent agreement in most discussions among political and social scientists that we can ignore distinctions and proceed on the assumption that everything can eventually be called anything else, and that distinctions are meaningful only to the extent that each of us has the right 'to define his terms.'" Asserting the power of her own distinction making, she presented totalitarianism as what the great sociologist Max Weber (a friend of Karl Jaspers's) had called an Ideal Type, distinguishing totalitarianism's Ideal Type from those of both tyranny and authoritarianism, and using metaphors to illuminate each. A totalitarian regime, she explained, is like a many-layered onion with an empty center where the leader is located; it is thus quite unlike the other regimes, which are structured like pyramids: the tyrannical pyramid wherein the leader, located on top, rules the people without intervening structures of authority, and the authoritarian one, wherein the leader rules through authority structures. "All the extraordinary manifold parts of the [onionlike totalitarian] movement: the front organizations, the various professional societies, the party membership, the party bureaucracy, the elite formations and police groups, are related in such a way that each forms the façade in one direction and the center in the other, that is, plays the role of normal outside world for one layer and the role of radical extremism for another. . . . The onion structure makes the system organizationally shock-proof against the factuality of the world."[8] Even though she was afraid that her Ideal Types would be used by others as formulas for making propaganda rather than as criteria for guiding judgment, she used them herself to assess postwar regimes such as Mao's China, which she judged to be a mixed type, both totalistic and terroristic but without the onionlike organizational structure of the Nazi and Soviet regimes. China's government seemed to her less able to encompass the entire country and less able to operate supranationally (and thus threaten Southeast Asia as the "domino theory" adherents in the United States assumed) than other regimes.

These revisions and refinements to *Origins* heralded Arendt's shift through the late 1950s and into the 1960s toward an exploration of the revolutionary traditions in Europe and America, with their revolutionary councils, as Ideal Types. This later work (which I shall discuss below) was of great importance for the student movements of the late 1960s in America and Europe, but so was *Eichmann in Jerusalem,* which also became, in effect, part of the unfolding story of *The Origins of Totalitarianism,* especially when she revised the latter yet again, in 1968. Her controversial conclusion that Eichmann was a banal man who thoughtlessly obeyed his Führer's will and reflected the debased German moral environment, along with her reflections on how the Nazis had manipulated the Judenräte (Jewish Councils), also spilled over into the furor that surrounded Rolf Hochhuth's play *The Deputy* (1963), which asked why Pope Pius XII had remained silent when he learned of the Nazi camps.[9] It was *Eichmann in Jerusalem,* however, that became in Germany the manual for the youth movement of 1968 as the new generation tried to make a break with the generation of their Nazi fathers.

By the end of the 1960s, the possibility that totalitarianism—in the midcentury form she had analyzed—would recur was no longer Arendt's galvanizing fear or her sole criterion for political judgment. *Origins* was reissued in 1968 as three books, corresponding to the three parts of the original, *Antisemitism, Imperialism, Totalitarianism.* Each contained a new preface describing the political realities of the late-1960s world. The *Totalitarianism* preface discussed the "detotalitarianizing" of the Soviet Union, its return to political purposes, national interests, and a late-twentieth-century form of intrusion into contiguous lands ("continental" imperialism) in Eastern Europe and Central Asia; Arendt saw this new Soviet imperialism as the counterpart of the economic continental imperialism being practiced by the United States, particularly in Latin America. Some forty years later, her preface can still show us how important it is to explore the diverse types of imperialism that arose in the nineteenth and twentieth centuries and to ask with open minds what forms imperialism takes now.

In the five years before her death, Arendt was working on what became the posthumously published three-volume *Life of the Mind*, which contains her last commentary on *The Origins of Totalitarianism*. *The Life of the Mind* begins with a philosophical as well as political investigation of Eichmann's thoughtlessness, the banality of the evildoer. As she had watched the man at his trial, she noted, a question had "imposed itself" on her—one she could no more escape than she could avoid her awareness of his role in running the concentration camps: "Could the activity of thinking as such, the habit of examining whatever comes to pass or attracts attention, regardless of results and specific content, could this activity be among the conditions that make men abstain from evildoing, or even actually 'condition' them against it?"[10] The long train of thought that had unfolded from her *analyses* of totalitarian and nontotalitarian elements had shifted to the *prevention* of evildoing.

I shall return to Arendt's last philosophical reflections on the banality of evil, but what I want to emphasize for the moment is how, in the slow process of composition and revision, the field-manual aspect of *The Origins of Totalitarianism* intensified. In each successive edition Arendt further distilled her insights into the elements of totalitarianism, illuminating the processes by which such elements could crystallize into totalitarianism. It is those elements and processes that I want to survey now, bearing in mind a comment in the 1968 edition of *Origins*—the one that Morgenthau's class was reading in 1971, during the Vietnam War. Her comment appeared in the essay "Ideology and Terror," in which she revealed that her current perspective on the *limits* of totalitarianism had enabled her to regard the world after the Soviet "thaw" and the Hungarian Revolution not as a place where totalitarianism might arise again in its midcentury forms but as a scene where the still existing elements of totalitarianism would be more likely to crystallize into *new* forms. "It may even be that the true predicaments of our time will assume their authentic form—though not necessarily the cruelest—only when totalitarianism has become a thing of the past."[11] This comment can stand as a prophecy: the elements of totalitarianism *have* continued to be with us, even in the most secure democracies, but they no longer take their mid-twentieth-century forms.

The first element of totalitarianism discussed in the field manual is the existence of an ideology that explains all of history and justifies the regime and its policies: a kind of "supersense." This ideology seems perfectly logical to those who subscribe to it and reason from its premises, which are far removed from reality. The ideology designates a superior people and an internal enemy (usually operating as a conspiracy) that must be eliminated. Gradually, the ideology comes to usurp all other foundations for the regime's legal system. Arendt described an ideology of Nature (particularly "natural" races) in Nazism and an ideology of History (particularly focused in a Marxian manner on class struggle and violent revolution) in Stalinism. In a totalitarian society the "methods of domination rest on the assumption that men can be completely conditioned because they are only functions of some higher historical or natural forces."[12] It is this functionalism that remains as a deep legacy in "the life of the mind."

The totalitarian denial of any laws other than ideological dictates coincided with (but was not caused by) the collapse of belief in any source of rights or actual laws outside of human nature itself—that is, the collapse of appeals to God as the source of laws in the monotheistic traditions or to "natural law" in the tradition of the French revolutionaries and their modern heirs or even to the idea that human beings were themselves the measure of all things human. Ideologies grew up in a secularizing world, but an ideology is not, as Arendt was very clear (and argued very clearly in a 1954 essay, "Religion and Politics"), a "secular religion." Despite some scholarly arguments, communism did not perform the same function for its adherents that various religions performed in free societies, and it did not arise out of a breakdown of Christian religious authority. The ideology of communism, on the contrary, required that religious experience be completely absent from the state, in which religious institutions were banned; it demonstrated that religious experience would eventually, as history unfolded, become unnecessary—it would wither away with the state.

As Arendt pointed out, the "free world" standing opposed to communism in the 1950s was one in which Christian churches were free from politics, able "to be and remain outside the realm of secular society altogether, something unheard of in the ancient world"; "The only interest Christianity has in secular government is to protect its own freedom, to see to it that the powers-that-be permit, among other freedoms, freedom from politics. The free world, however, means by freedom not 'Render unto Caesar what is Caesar's and unto God what is God's,' but the right of all to handle those affairs that were once Caesar's. The very fact that we, as far as our public life is concerned, care more about freedom than about anything else proves that we do not live publicly in a religious world."[13]

Arendt did not subscribe to the theoretical notion, put forward so forcefully by Marx, that a religion is an ideology, one among many possible ideologies, a "superstructure" or mental product comparable to a product made in a factory. But she was aware that this functionalist view of religion had become woven into social science, and that it was difficult for contemporary intellectuals to grasp that authentic religions are not of the political world, either of a free world that permits them or of a totalitarian world that suppresses them.

By the same token, Arendt did not explicitly consider the possibility that religious ideologies might develop, that is, that religious people living in nation-states might want their religions to become nationally or supranationally political. She was aware, of course, that there were religious nationalist parties in almost every multiparty country (such as Adenauer's Christian Nationalist Party), and she had certainly many times pointed out in the 1950s the danger of Israel's having been founded as a Jewish state, making all the political parties, in effect, to varying degrees, Jewish nationalist parties. But she did not anticipate what we have witnessed since her death: the unprecedented upsurge of political religions that occurred when the world order secured by the standoff between the United States and the Soviet Union collapsed in 1989 along with the Berlin Wall. The so-called fundamentalisms that have emerged, with their very different histories, are perversions of Christianity and Islam: they are, in Arendt's terms, no longer authentic religions but adaptations of religions for supranational political purposes and as such they perform many of the functions that the mid-twentieth-century ideologies of Nature and History did.

Further, these religious ideologies both grow from and foster the kind of supersense that had characterized the totalitarian ideologies. For those who subscribe to them, religious ideologies have an irrefutable logic, one that makes no sense to nonbelievers because the premises are not of the common world and not related to common sense. In Arendt's view political judgment begins from things, people, or events as they appear in the world and then moves toward general statements. It develops "reflectively" in Kant's terms, not "deductively." A political judgment is expressed as an opinion. But neither philosophers (with exceptions, like Kant and Jaspers) nor religious ideologues respect opinion; the philosophers say opinion has nothing to do with absolute truth, and religious people (both authentically religious people and ideologues) respect only revealed Truth. The fact that free political organizations, small and large, stand on the authority of opinion, preserving freedom for the exchange of opinions, debate, and argument, makes them anathema to those who look for authority beyond the common world. It was for this reason that Max Weber noted, succinctly, "There is no arguing with religious warriors."

In the parts of the world where there is little separation of church and state, or where such a separation is eroding (as it is now in America), religious beliefs are easily perverted into political instruments. Religions that were not imperialistic in the early twentieth century have become so. In America, Christian fundamentalists announce "crusades" for democracy, and across the Middle East Islamic fundamentalists proclaim "the new caliphate." As a religious state, Israel has had a religious legacy to defend (now with nuclear weapons capacity) ever since its founding in 1948, when the necessity to create a Jewish state was used to justify making refugees of all the non-Jewish residents of Palestine. The legacy became supranationalist among advocates of a "Greater Israel" who sanctioned the stateless condition of the refugees. Iran has become once again, as it was under Ayatollah Khomeini, a Shiite one-party authoritarian dictatorship, but now its leaders dangerously rant about "throwing all the Jews into the sea" or forcing Israel to set up a state in Europe and give way to the Palestinians. The Iranian religious government has not, however, completely suppressed its secular citizens or its electoral process, nor has it espoused supranational land grabbing —which is why those in Europe and the United Nations who call for diplomacy to keep Teheran from further extremism and militarization are so right, and those in America who threaten to invade it on such a dangerous crusade are so wrong.

A second key element of totalitarianism is total terror, which Arendt saw essentially institutionalized in the Nazi concentration camps and the Soviet labor camps. Ultimately sparing no part of the population, total terror was preceded in these regimes by the dissolution of traditional class structures and political allegiances in a fervent political "movement" that eventually made the uprooting and moving of huge populations in their mass societies seem necessary and justifiable. Arendt also noted that the introduction in 1945 of atomic weapons put the world under threat of a new form of total terror, which meant new institutions for wielding that threat would become necessary if new forms of totalitarianism adopted them. But no matter what the form, it is the *total* in total terror that is key. Once willingness to persecute and sacrifice huge numbers of people, whole subpopulations, to the logic of an ideology (that is, for no practical or strategic reason) had appeared in history, it could not go away. This destruction is no longer "unthinkable." It is all too thinkable—or all too invocable by the thoughtless. Total terror or total war has been with us, a disease in uncertain remission, for more than fifty years.

At the outset of the Cold War, leaders of the superpowers possessing nuclear weapons subscribed to the maxim that wartime leaders like Eisenhower and Churchill had articulated and even the volatile Khrushchev had accepted, namely, that the potentiality of nuclear holocaust meant that war should not be an instrument of policy, for there was no middle ground between total war and no war. But this rule did not hold for long, and by the mid-1960s, after the Cuban Missile Crisis, when the Vietnam War was escalating and various middle-ground wars were kindled around the world, the no-war rule—despite treaties banning nuclear testing—was accepted neither in Washington nor in Moscow, and it was completely ignored in states where nuclear weapons had proliferated and often buttressed authoritarian regimes. Nuclear testing and threats of "limited" nuclear war have not been rare since. And we have recently seen how thought-paralyzing even an accusation that a state might have nuclear weapons can be. The breakdown of the doctrine of nuclear deterrence and the proliferation of nuclear weapons into nonsuperpower hands have set the stage for the current wave of terrorism that knows no national borders and for a general move toward violence in politics. As early as 1950 Arendt had reflected on Carl von Clausewitz's famous dictum that war is the continuation of politics by other means with the chilling observation: "It seems more true to put this dictum in reverse: Politics is the continuation of war by other means."[14] She was fully aware that the less commitment there is in the world to politics, which ultimately means to sharing the earth with other peoples, the more temptation there is to violence and terrorism.

Arendt identified as a third element of totalitarianism the destruction of natural human bonds, chiefly of the family, accomplished by laws regulating marriage (and forbidding marriage between peoples designated superior and those designated inferior). Bonds can also be assaulted by police practices that force people to spy on and inform on family members. Along with the destruction of public spaces—the destruction of politics—in a totalitarian regime goes the destruction of private spaces for intimacy and family life.

Today the invasion of private spaces by ideological agencies (both governmental and religious) takes two important forms in national settings of diverse sorts. The first is the use of school systems for ideological indoctrination. In the United States school curricula have become a key battleground for Christian proselytizers, who lobby for public financing of religious education; while in many areas of the world with predominant Muslim populations religious schools are the only schools allowed (and they are only for males). The history of imperialism is still being falsely taught in areas where the legacy of the mid-twentieth-century totalitarianisms lives on. In Japan, to choose an example from outside the sphere of religious ideologies, history textbooks deny Japan's imperialism of the 1890s, which resulted in the brutal colonization of Korea; the same textbooks omit Japan's invasion of northeast China during the Second World War, which resulted in an estimated ten million civilian deaths. Regulation of marriage and reproduction, another area of ideological manipulation that is particularly acute in states where religious ideologies reign, is used now not just to segregate groups labeled inferior but to maintain control over women and sexual minorities.

But the regulation of family life in contemporary settings has a further consequence that is just as damaging to human bonds as the older regulatory methods were. Particularly in parts of the world where family structures are changing rapidly and where the portion of the population under the age of twenty is steadily increasing, generational bonds are consistently abused or broken to control the young or press them into political service on a scale that makes the Nazi Youth Movement appear amateurish. Around the world, children are forced into adult roles, whether as soldiers or prostitutes or prisoners or heads of families (many of the now 15 million AIDS orphans). Worse, many of these children are stateless. The U.N. children's agency UNICEF estimates that 50 million children a year are neither registered nor provided with a legal identity at birth—a number that dwarfs the number of people made stateless during the Second World War.[15] Many of the crimes against children—against the humanity of children—are crimes, as it were, of omission rather than commission: children are not provided with the minimum conditions necessary for normal development. They are deprived of childhood. But wherever children are unable to thrive and are not formally recognized, there are no future citizens being created, no "new beginnings" (in Arendt's term) being fostered, and this "childism" (as the prejudice might be called) is a kind of incipient totalitarianism without borders.

Government by bureaucracy was a fourth element of totalitarianism that Arendt identified, tracking its history from the nineteenth-century imperial regimes and examining its assault upon individual judgment and responsibility as it became in Germany and the Soviet Union "government by nobody." She also identified as elements the domination of the totalitarian regimes by their secret police, rather than their national armies, and the corruption of their legal institutions, particularly those designed to protect the private and political spaces (free speech, free press, right of assembly, and so on). The totalitarian governments also asserted their absolute sovereignty and thereby justified continental imperialism into lands with peoples claimed as *Volk* in the biological or historical terms asserted in their ideology. (Arendt's critique of sovereignty is a little-known feature of her work, to which I shall return in detail below.)

In identifying these last elements of totalitarianism, Arendt was also elaborating upon one of the basic processual insights of *The Origins of Totalitarianism,* which was that the nineteenth-century overseas imperialists—the European states that colonized Africa, the Middle East, and parts of Asia—exported to those lands their own superfluous people, their déclassé mobs, where they were overseen by a type of colonialist bureaucrat who became accustomed to treating the mob and the colonized peoples as subhumans and trampling upon their local laws and customs. She argued that these imperialist methods in turn corrupted the European states themselves, which carried the methods over into their continental imperialisms. Both Germany and Russia, in effect, made colonials out of their own unwanted populations: their Jews, their dissidents. The concentration camp and the labor camp had their prototypes in the Bantustans of South Africa.

This reap-what-you-sow process or "hidden mechanism" helped crystallize totalitarian elements into full-blown totalitarian regimes. That is, methods protototalitarians practiced upon foreign "others" came closer to home as they became a way of life. The habit of dehumanizing, of thinking of human beings in terms of functions, eventually redounded upon fellow nationals at home and even, finally, upon the totalitarians themselves (as, for instance, when Hitler started eliminating inferior "Aryans" and his own troops, or when Stalin began purging his own professional classes). Arendt was aware, too, that those fighting against totalitarians for whom "everything is permitted" can easily be drawn into totalitarian methods, as the Allied armies of World War II began ignoring the distinction between combatants and civilians and bombed nonmilitary German and Japanese cities in 1945. In Japan an estimated 160,000 people were directly killed in a day, and there was no real national debate in America—then or since— over this result. By the time, twenty years later, when the United States came to fight a protracted war in Vietnam, the U.S. government considered the bombing and napalming of civilians acceptable practice. This was one of the developments that made Hans Morgenthau resign his National Security position in protest. By now few people complain at the routine labeling of civilian deaths during the American invasions of Afghanistan and Iraq as "collateral damage." It is not abnormal to think that the end justifies the means, for what else but an end would justify a means? But it is obvious that when this kind of thinking becomes the only kind of thinking the means will become, over time, the end.

Since the mid-1990s it has also become apparent that one of the most threatening ways that adopting totalitarian methods to fight totalitarianism helped shape the current world order was in the practice adopted by U.S. governments during the Cold War period of sponsoring Islamic fundamentalists as agents of opposition to Soviet communism. This began on a small scale during Eisenhower's presidency with support for the Muslim Brotherhood led by the Egyptian Hassan al-Banna, a group that had developed far-flung offshoots throughout the Middle East and on the Indian subcontinent, including some twenty-five units in Palestine that joined in fighting the Jewish army in 1948. In Washington it was originally hoped that the political Islamists would help prevent the Communist ideology from infecting the Arab states, but the policy of support became progressively aimed more at promoting Arab supranationalism and funding middle-ground wars. U.S. support of Arab supranationalism (with its own ideology, Wahhabism) focused on the reactionary Saudi monarchy, which was encouraged to create a network of right-wing Arab states using the Muslim Brotherhood as its agent. The Saudis also built on the Brotherhood's violent opposition to Egypt under Nasser, who was considered a revolutionary nationalist in Washington and posed a direct challenge to U.S. and British oil interests in the Gulf.

With America's help, violence was spread throughout the Brotherhood membership by means of the CIA, which, in the most portentous instance, supported the Afghan fighters in their resistance to the Soviet Union's imperialist invasion of Afghanistan in the 1980s. At that time, the CIA helped Osama bin Laden build a network of "Afghan Arabs," the forerunner of al-Qaeda. Meanwhile, the Taliban in Afghanistan were nurtured by Pakistani Islamists modeling themselves on the Muslim Brotherhood; they in turn supported al-Qaeda throughout the 1990s while it was starting to aim its terrorist attacks at "the West" and the very hands that had fed it.

Even while she was completing *The Origins of Totalitarianism* and then beginning to observe how her book was received during the international struggle of the Cold War, Arendt was starting to revise her understanding of several of the elements of totalitarianism that I have just outlined. She was spurred by new realities of two sorts: memoirs emerging both from Germany and, especially, from survivors of the Soviet camps; and the way in which the American political system, secured by its citizens' respect for their strong Constitution, responded to McCarthyism.

The survivors' memoirs taught her that even in the defining institution of totalitarianism, the camps, politics does not disappear completely; the "holes of oblivion" are not holes of complete oblivion. This fact fitted with the claim she had made in her "Concluding Remarks" that the totalitarian "contempt for utilitarian motives," the vast denial of reality and commonsense characteristic of totalitarians fixated on ideologically defined goals, had a built-in limit as long as the regime was not global. The totalitarians, overreaching themselves, generated resistance and opposition among people not infected with their supersense, particularly in the lands they set out to conquer as quickly—and impractically—as possible. "[One] should bear in mind the necessary limitations to an experiment which requires global control in order to show conclusive results. Until now the totalitarian belief that everything is possible seems to have proved only that everything can be destroyed."[16]

In conceptual terms, Arendt realized that as long as human plurality is not completely destroyed, as long as people's identities and actions are not utterly suppressed, new beginnings are possible. Seeing plurality as what essentially must be preserved against totalitarian threats, she could frame the task of doing so with clarity. First, she offered the totalitarian regimes as agents of instruction, demonstrating by means of their unprecedented institution, the concentration camps, the possibility of previously unimaginable things: "Yet in their effort to prove that everything is possible, totalitarian regimes have discovered without knowing it that there are crimes which men can neither punish nor forgive. When the impossible was made possible it became the unpunishable, unforgivable absolute evil which could no longer be understood and explained by the evil motives of self-interest, greed, covetousness, resentment, lust for power, and cowardice; and which therefore anger could not revenge, love could not endure, friendship could not forgive. Just as the victims in the death factories or the holes of oblivion are no longer 'human' in the eyes of their executioners, so this newest species of criminals is beyond the pale even of solidarity in human sinfulness."[17]

Even though after the Eichmann trial Arendt stopped speaking of absolute or radical evil and referred to "the banality of evil" to describe the criminals, she did not give up her claim that the novel crimes—those called at the Nuremberg Trials "crimes against humanity"—involved denying human plurality, which in legal terms did not mean denying human beings any specific rights but denying them the right to have rights. From Arendt's point of view, a crime against humanity is one that assaults the right to belong to a human community: the right not to be reduced to a mass, not to be made superfluous, not to be stateless and rightless. It is the right to be remembered truthfully in stories told about plural human beings by plural human beings, not to be erased from history. "Crimes against humanity" might be defined in Arendtian terms as crimes against human plurality, and to judge them as such one needs to prove not a motive to genocide but only a motive to deny plurality, for example, by making a group stateless. (By this criterion, the uprooting and devastation of black African populations now in course in Darfur is a crime against humanity and should be prosecuted as such, without waiting for the numbers of dead to reach Rwandan proportions so it can officially be called "genocide.") Without specifying its form, Arendt was appealing in the "Concluding Remarks" to a "consciously devised new polity"—a "consciously planned beginning of history" that would protect human plurality in new ways.[18]

While I have been presenting *The Origins of Totalitarianism* as a field manual, I have also been alluding to some of the forms that the elements of totalitarianism have taken in our world. I want now to come directly to this topic. It seems to me that there are three themes of Arendt's book that can be particularly useful for us to consider while we try to think our way through to some clarity about what has happened since the fall of the Berlin Wall and, more recently, the attacks on the World Trade Center and the Pentagon. These attacks led to the beginning of the so-called war on terror, which defines the present political moment and weighs so heavily against the hopefulness engendered by the end of the Cold War.

The first theme is the one with which I opened this book: novelty in human affairs. I have tried to show that as she wrote and revised her book, Arendt disciplined herself to a habit of political analysis that she maintained throughout the rest of her life. She made distinctions and worked to conceptualize ideas clearly, inquiring into the historical meaning and the present usefulness of each concept she explored, starting with "totalitarianism" itself. In considering any current political event or question, she thought it particularly important—as had Thucydides in writing his history of the Peloponnesian War during its unfolding—to distinguish what was familiar and already conceptualized from what was new and just becoming conceptualizable, and thus discussable, part of political conversation. So when she made the claim that totalitarianism was a novel form of government, distinct from such familiar forms as tyranny, oligarchy, and democracy, Arendt took it as her responsibility to say, carefully and thoroughly, what was "unprecedented" about it. (She always used this word with utmost rigor, particularly after the Eichmann Controversy, when it became one of the most hackneyed terms in our political vocabulary.) Opposing a totalitarian regime effectively, Arendt understood, required isolating the features that made this form of government novel. As I suggested, political analysis for her was less a matter of culling lessons from the past than of being able to identify what was new, which calls for a new, creative response.

Let me start my consideration of this first theme by noting that the American public response to the "Attack on America" got off to an understandably stunned but also unthinking start. President George W. Bush and an instantly united Congress called the attack an act of war, and they, in turn, declared war. Pearl Harbor was constantly invoked. But at the same time it was immediately clear that the United States was declaring war without having an enemy state or even (at first) a nonstate group claiming responsibility. There was no Japan behind those lethal hijacked planes, nor even (at first) an identifiable criminal or terrorist perpetrator. So Americans were called upon to ready for a "war on terrorism," which is as impersonal a phrase as "war on drugs" and far more dangerous; when no enemies are named, the door is open to limitless war outside of all rules of war. The president next felt compelled to proclaim any state harboring terrorists America's enemy, in a futile effort to find a state to stand in for the missing Japan. Afghanistan became the target; as a state with an army, it was said to be the enemy, although it was certainly not the Taliban that attacked the United Sates. But in the days after the Attack on America, many Americans came to the realization (long familiar among intelligence communities) that every state in the world (including the United States) harbors terrorists, whether it directly supports them or not, and that many terrorists have affinities or active networks across state borders, even across the borders of their specific ideologies.

That there are interconnected terrorist cells and training programs all over the world now is not news, and even the attack on the World Trade Center was not, of course, unprecedented. There had been an earlier attack in 1993. The weapon—suicide bombers bearing explosives—is not new, only horrifyingly expanded to involve planes full of civilians, not just single kamikazes. Americans were witnessing the proud achievements of their own technology turned with logistical mastery upon them by men who despised Western technological achievements as morally corrupting. But it seems to me that what is novel about the event will become clearer if we look at the response to it and consider how that response illuminated the dynamics of contemporary terrorism both to ordinary people and to the intelligence agents.

The response to the attacks was without precedent on several levels. First, on the level of international politics, NATO invoked for the first time its "one, all" doctrine: America's allies rallied immediately to engage in discussions about a coordinated action. They were much more ready than the members of the U.S. Congress to be political, that is, to discuss and debate publicly what action would be appropriate, rather than to sign on for war behind the American president. Nation-states that had maintained adversarial relations with the United States were prompted to cooperate or stepped forward voluntarily, as did, unexpectedly, both Russia and China, the legatees of mid-twentieth-century totalitarianisms. No one knew how or whether these new alliances would hold, but they raised possibilities for profound change in the world order. The moment was potentially a revolutionary one on an international scale, something that had not existed since the fall of the Berlin Wall. If the U.S. government had been able to embrace the idea of coordinated action among these nations, and potentially others as well, or if the American president had been able to overcome the traditional American aversion to giving up any sovereignty and turned to the United Nations as the agency through which to debate the issue and coordinate a response, what Arendt called "mutual promises" might have resulted.

But the second unprecedented feature of the response weighed heavily against the first. National security became instantaneously the U.S. government's priority. The nation—not just the crime scenes or the city of New York—became, overnight, militarized and policed in a way it had never been previously, and the number of drastic security measures proposed, many challenging existing laws and the right to privacy, went beyond responses to previous terrorist attacks. A huge governmental reorganization brought the Department of Homeland Security into existence, vastly extending the scope of the Executive Branch of the government, while the secret services began to operate like a shadow government, that is, in ways that Arendt had identified as proto-totalitarian during the McCarthy era and the Vietnam War.

Third, and more difficult to describe, was the subjective response that developed after September 11: the nearly unanimous claim (or feeling) that a historical chasm had opened in the world, not just in the United States. In newspapers and in the talk of people worldwide, the headline was the same: this was "The Day the World Changed" (as the *Economist*'s cover put it). From the Middle East many voices chided the Americans, taunting, "See, now you know what it is to live with terrorism." But people everywhere were struggling to understand why this threat to the world seemed deeper than anything posed by terrorism before. It seemed more threatening even than the 1962 Cuban Missile Crisis, because an actual attack—played and replayed on television— rather than a doomsday scenario, was at stake. For the first time, people around the world grasped concretely that the material and social conditions of modern life mean that a terrorist attack on this scale—or even more deadly, with biological, chemical, or nuclear means—could take place at any moment. It wasn't even necessary to have an enemy state acting as agent. The radicalness of the anxiety aroused by this attack was unprecedented as the contemporary form of total terror stood revealed.

It is important to recognize that this radical insecurity is connected to the fact that the attack was *not* an act of war, despite President Bush's terminology. Calling it an act of war made it familiar, aligned it with an image of war as it had been before the Cold War, an image that ruled out as "unthinkable" a nuclear war aimed at the elimination of the warring parties and all battlefields. To call the attack an act of war was to connect it *wishfully* with the pre-nuclear Pearl Harbor attack, which launched Americans into a worldwide but still limited war they could win. Wars were considered winnable, and the definitions of war in place then permitted the "free world" acts that were far more devastating than what happened on September 11. Fighting totalitarian Germany and its ally Japan, American planes killed hundreds of thousands of civilians with fire bombs and atom bombs—and these deeds were held to be justified because the United States was at war and trying to bring the war to a victorious end as quickly as possible. It is painful to think that the Allied bombings of civilians then became part of a worldwide erosion of the distinction between civilians and combatants. This blurring of human boundaries has so changed the nature of war that now there is no morally or politically defensible way to say of a war with staggering civilian loss that you have "won." So the Attack on America reminds us that since the end of World War II we have all lived in a world in which civilians are routinely targets, and any act of violence—in the context of a declared war or not—can become an uncontainable conflagration of civilians.

Further, the September 11th attack reminded Americans that they faced an enemy against whom they could not, from the outset, wage an army-to-army war. A terrorist network is not a state that can be attacked with a crippling missile fusillade as Iraq was in the First Gulf War. So as it prepared for the invasion of Afghanistan, the Bush administration shifted historical analogy: Secretary of Defense Rumsfeld stopped talking about Pearl Harbor and started talking about a new Cold War, a long war that would, after its initial phase, take place mostly off the world's TV screens. (He was, in effect, announcing the program of illegal arrests, torture, and renditions that has come into being since.) To a certain extent, American leaders seemed to recognize that killing or making refugees out of large numbers of civilians who are nationals of a state, Afghanistan, that was not the object of their declaration of war "against terrorism" would turn America into the unjustified aggressor, paving the way for yet another generation of terrorists of many different nationalities with yet more reasons to hate the United States and its allies, "the West." Nonetheless, President Bush threatened to "eradicate" the terrorists because it was obvious that unless they were eradicated they or their protégés would strike again.

But even as he spoke, the few opponents of the invasion warned that these terrorist networks could not be eradicated by military invasion, not even if all Afghanistan were laid waste (any more than a guerrilla army woven into the geographical and social fabric of Vietnam was eradicable through thousands of bombing raids). Further, if all of Afghanistan were to be laid waste, the war would become unlimited in the sense that other states in the region, flooded with refugees and stirred to sympathy for the victimized Afghans, would be (as the strategists say) destabilized. All these possibilities were considered again as the Bush administration prepared in 2003 for the preemptive attack on Iraq, a terrifying new precedent, which was justified by the claim that Saddam Hussein had weapons of mass destruction (WMD) ready to turn upon his neighbors and upon "the West." But the debate, engaged by unprecedentedly large numbers of demonstrators worldwide, in cities and towns (organized and coordinated by use of the Internet), remained muted in Washington, as Congress bowed to the commander-in-chief. The checks and balances of the American republican tradition were threatened more decisively than in any previous military operation.

Trying to make the terrorist network identifiable, the Bush administration and the media concentrated on the figure of Osama bin Laden, still at large five years after the war against Afghanistan. He is described as "the mastermind," and constantly analogized to Hitler and Stalin. Focusing so much attention on him has handed him power, bolstering his reputation in the Islamic world, a reputation to which the Clinton administration had already given a boost in 1998 with its useless aerial attack on Afghanistan. Bin Laden himself has made it clear in interviews that were he to be killed, another and yet another bin Laden would come forth to take his place. He is not a Hitler or a Stalin; his organization is completely different from a state-based or governmental totalitarian regime of the sort that Arendt compared to an onion. There are no layers of bureaucracy, and his followers are not bureaucrats, banally dedicated to their roles as state agents. This organization is a web, nearly invisible, its strands connected but not centralized by the worldwide links of an electronic communications network. This network of hundreds of organizations, existing wherever there are Muslim populations, takes as its collective name "The World Islamic Front" in recognition of earlier revolutionary movements, but there is no front to the Front, and this is not a social or politically revolutionary movement; it is a bid for *restoration* of Muslim purity.

The U.S. government's response, to prepare for a war that had a purpose—eradicating terrorism—that could not be achieved by war, has made clear what the new organizational feature of this terrorism is: it *explicitly* does not serve politics. This is not terrorism within a state or territory designed to rectify a national injustice or to protest a government, like the terrorism of the Irish Republican Army or (in the realm of fantasized national injustices) the American Nazi-like antigovernment militias. It is not terrorism in the service of national liberation, although some of the organizations involved in the World Islamic Front—particularly in Egypt—do have as a goal taking over a specific state government they feel has been corrupted. It is not terrorism in the service of an aspiration to have a state, like the Palestinian *intifada*. It is not state-sponsored terrorism, although some states give it aid. Finally, it is not what in the 1970s and 1980s was known as "international terrorism," in which terrorists move and unite across state boundaries in the manner of the Red Brigade, carrying out kidnappings and assassinations to make a political statement by violent means. This is an unprecedented form of terrorism involving people (almost all male) of many nationalities, living in their own or other states, united by a supranational purpose that is explicitly *antipolitical*. Arendt had identified total terror as a necessary element of totalitarianism, and this is its novel form.

The second theme of *The Origins of Totalitarianism* I wish to discuss is the emphasis on supranationalism and antipolitical purposes. In the last decades of the nineteenth century and into the twentieth-century era of totalitarianisms, Arendt tracked a huge tension between two basic political aspirations. On the one hand, people want to create nation-states, that is, states uniting into a legal entity people of some homogeneity, connected by origin or what the French called *nationalité*. The revolutionary fervor of the nineteenth century focused on breaking down monarchies and empires and founding limited constitutional states, secular states. On the other hand, there were many people, particularly in Europe, who wanted the newly constituted or reconstituted states to extend their political and economic reach beyond state borders. Two forms of state-sponsored imperialism arose, to which Arendt gave the names overseas imperialism and continental imperialism. Most of the European nation-states set up overseas colonial regimes in Africa, the Middle East, and Asia, refusing any legal protections to the colonized peoples and ruthlessly exploiting them and their resources. Meanwhile, in two regions where full-blown totalitarian regimes eventually evolved, ideologues invoked Pan-German and Pan-Slavic supernations, using ideological mystifications about the German and the Slavic souls that later fueled the Nazi programs for eliminating non-Aryans and the Stalinist mass murders, labor camps, and purges.

The tension between national and supranational aspirations took many forms. But it was clear to Arendt that totalitarianisms were the products of supranationalism triumphant. Supranationalism is not the linking of limited states into a union—a federation or confederation, a united states—it is, rather, the dissolving of limited constitutional forms into an amorphous bonding of people, a racially defined *Volk* or a theoretically defined worldwide proletariat or—we see the potential now—a religiously defined militia of the devout. The ideology that fuels a supranationalist and potentially totalitarian movement calls for the elimination of elected congresses and courts and for the adoption of something vaguely energetic, like the Führer's will. Or Allah's will, as represented by his self-appointed agents, which is how Osama bin Laden and his many similars represent themselves. The aspiration of their Islamic movement is to bring down the governments that have betrayed their Muslim populations by collaborating with the secularizing infidels of the West and to make a holy war upon those governments and peoples of the West—combatants and civilians without distinction—who have assaulted Muslims and desecrated Muslim holy sites and lands. In interviews, bin Laden has envisioned a supranational unity of devout, uncorrupted Muslims, a pan-Muslimism that has no political shape or form, not even the theocratic government by clerics that has taken national form in Iran. His image is of Allah speaking directly through the Quran to all his dedicated soldiers, dictating every action of their daily lives—a kind of "democratic" supranationalism.

Arendt thought that the key criterion for judging whether a group or a regime was moving in the direction of totalitarianism was the kind and form its supranationalism took. She would, for example, have taken the measure of Slobodan Milošević's government from his talk about "Greater Serbia," a phrase he obviously and purposefully modeled on Hitler's "Greater Germany." The appropriation among the Serb supranationalists of the techniques of mid-twentieth-century totalitarian terror—the measures of "ethnic cleansing," the mass killings of civilians, and the concentration camps—were the clearest evidence that this was a government dedicated to the destruction of all political life in Serbia and all the populations (especially the Muslims) of the lands claimed as Greater Serbia. The midcentury model of totalitarianism that Milošević followed was of a state growing over its borders, a continental imperialism driven by a state administration, with Muslims cast in the role of the obsessional focal point of hatred that the Jews had been given in the Nazi ideology. At his trial, and to the day he died, Milošević was unrepentant in the Nazi manner, for his ideology provided him with irrefutable supersense. But his state administration, reflecting years of underdevelopment under Marshal Tito, lacked the resources, economic and technological, to develop the full onionlike totalitarian layering on even a relatively small scale.

What we see in the terrorist networks for which Osama bin Laden and others supply the ideological rhetoric is a supranationalism that does not presume a state administration. Allah's operatives are planning not to round up populations into camps or killing centers but to create terror of the sort that the United States has just experienced—the extraterritorial terror that is open to those who do not have a homeland or a "Greater X" to serve. Bin Laden sometimes speaks of "the Islamic nation," or "the nation of Muhammad," but this is a supranation founded on an interpretation of Scripture. As Osama bin Laden declares in every interview, "We expect to be rewarded by Allah."[19]

If we turn Arendt's criteria about supranationalism upon America, as she did in the McCarthy era and during the Vietnam War, we should note that even before September 11, the Bush administration was engaged in a domestic policy of eroding civil liberties and undermining the separation of church and state, two of the elements of totalitarianism outlined by Arendt, though she noted that such elements can exist in many contexts without ever becoming totalitarian, just as elements of totalitarianism can come into existence in fighting totalitarianism, as happened in America during the McCarthy and Vietnam eras. The administration was also engaged before September 11 in a foreign policy that many commentators mistook for isolationism in the familiar American nationalistic manner. This involved withdrawing from established treaties and environmental accords, as well as from cooperation in the venue of the United Nations.

But this unilateralist policy, it seems to me, would be much more accurately described as an *antipolitics,* an attack upon existing alliances with the intention of clearing a path for a renewal and continuation of American overseas imperialism, which is largely economic and requires government by corporations or, to put it more bluntly, the buying of the government by corporate interests. This overseas imperialism, which had its expansionary heyday in the Reagan-Bush and even Clinton years, is precisely what Osama bin Laden sees as the enemy of Islam. This is "the

Crusader-Jewish alliance" that raided Muslim countries for oil, displaced Muslim populations, desecrated Muslim shrines, and backed corrupt regimes like that of the Saudi royal family or of Mubarak in Egypt and Suharto in Indonesia. The supranationalist ideological element that the U.S. leadership and the leadership of the terrorist network share is the proclivity to think in totalizing, world-historical good-versus-evil dualisms: the East versus the West, a "clash of civilizations." This dualism is equated either with spiritual virtue versus spiritual corruption or with authoritarian hatred of freedom versus love of freedom, depending on who is doing the name-calling.

The mere half a decade since the Attack on America, the opening of the era of the war on terrorism, has been dominated by a kind of regression into supranationalist aspiration after a twenty-year period, ushered in with the fall of the Berlin Wall, when the idea of what Arendt called "a comity of nations" was ascendant and an international human rights movement emerged. The European Union, a version of the federation of nations that Arendt had called for in all the editions of *The Origins of Totalitarianism,* was and is a repudiation of supranationalism. But in this regressive era, the problems of the European Union's constitution have surfaced, and they turn out to be international versions of the problems Arendt identified in *On Revolution,* where, in a discussion of national constitutions, she noted that the union's centralization and rulership could conflict with individual nation-state goals. At the same time, the human rights movement has been partially diverted into issues involving protection of the rights of citizens from security measures and the rights of suspected terrorists in prisons and detention centers, including state-sanctioned torture centers.

The third theme that Arendt concentrated on in *The Origins of Totalitarianism* concerned what she called "superfluous people" and the legacies of nineteenth-century imperialism. I think that the "Totalitarianism" section of *The Origins of Totalitarianism,* which deals with the transition from totalitarian movements to full-blown totalitarianism, total terror, and genocide, is probably the best known among political theorists. But it seems to me that in our present world situation the less-well-known "Imperialism" section is of equal importance. This section is full of passages in which Arendt's acquaintance with history outside Europe (particularly in Asia and Latin America) is obviously limited, but it is, nonetheless, also full of important reflections about the phenomenon we now call (vaguely) "globalization."

The differences among the late-nineteenth-century overseas and continental imperialisms of the European nation-states (and America), the imperialisms of the late-twentieth century, and those emergent now, which do not involve colonization, are key to understanding globalization, both its potential benefits for the planetary tribe and its potential dangers. Let me give just one example.

Arendt was prescient in her focus on the crucial role played by movements of population in the imperialism that followed the Industrial Revolution, which was spurred by mergers of governments and capitalists (state capitalism) for big, state-run projects like the building of the Panama and Suez Canals. Europe's "surplus populations" were shipped off to "dark" continents, providing the first key lesson in what being a "superfluous person" could mean, for the "superfluous" European exports treated the people they colonized as superfluous, transmitting, as it were, their trauma. Today, while middle managers and technicians are being exported to the developing world from the developed nations, war refugees and economic immigrants are coming into the developed nations by the millions, completely changing the demographies of Europe and America. Multicultural states are ending the era of relatively homogenous nation-states in ways that even a country like America, founded by immigrants, has little capacity to celebrate. The current overseas imperialists, not aspiring to rule governmentally over the indigenous populations, who are citizens of their own more-or-less stable new states, aspire instead to exploit their overseas resources and cheap labor; this is rule by corporations. But the result is that the cheap laborers, learning from the exploiters' tools—their televisions and telephones and computers—that material conditions are better in the exploiters' countries, aspire either to go to those countries or to become local agent-exploiters of their own fellow nationals. Now it is the postcolonial new states that have become state capitalist enterprises, massively corrupt and a breeding ground for both tyrants and terrorists. Currently, the most acute examples of this phenomenon are in western Africa.

Arendt showed clearly how late-nineteenth-century imperialism rebounded on the imperialists as the colonialists transmitted back to the state their ethic of ruthlessness, but we are only beginning to understand how exploitation can end up as the norm everywhere, rendering all kinds of groups "superfluous," not just ethnic or political groups but age groups like children and adolescents. These groups are not deprived of their rights as citizens; they never had legal status in the first place. Globalization certainly distributes some beneficial features of advanced technology, such as education, including education in political processes; it puts people in touch with one another, promoting a sense of humankind. But it also implicates the entire world in a mentality that—with an Eichmann-like indifference to life and death—identifies people as superfluous and leads to the imperialist techniques of ghettoization and massacre that Arendt portrayed.

two

The Human Condition and Actions That Matter

In her early commentaries on totalitarian elements that existed in the post-totalitarian world of the second half of the twentieth century, Arendt had, as I have said, a single question: Are these elements leading a state toward totalitarianism or not? But by the late 1950s, after the Soviet Union had repudiated Stalinism and McCarthyism had been discredited, she had progressed to a more general sense that totalitarian elements do not necessarily crystallize into a totalitarian state. So it became more important to put the positive side of the question: What elements can preserve freedom or help people achieve freedom?

She started writing enthusiastically about the history of political ideology and action, later focusing specifically on America's revolutionary history. In 1955 Jaspers, anticipating a visit from her that would bring him and his wife "the wide world," heard the new note directly after having observed for some time a diminishing of the anguish, fear, and rage that sounded throughout the years when she was writing *The Origins of Totalitarianism*. "Yes," she replied, "I would like to bring the wide world to you this time. I've begun so late, really only in recent years, to truly love the world, that I shall be able to do that now. Out of gratitude, I want to call my book on political theories 'Amor Mundi.'"[1]

The book she wrote, however, was called not *Amor Mundi* but *The Human Condition*. Published in 1958, it is a startling book: a bold, challenging theoretical lexicon, in which familiar words receive completely unfamiliar definitions. In it Arendt proposed nothing less than " a reconsideration of the human condition from the vantage point of our newest experiences and our most recent fears."[2] To think about "what we are doing" in a world of unprecedented technological advances and of post-totalitarian social and political formations, she put her emphasis on *how* we think about *what* we are doing and particularly on what inhibits us in our thinking. Are there ways of defining and ways of thinking—conceptual prejudices—that hinder us from appreciating the realities of the post-totalitarian world? You have to read the book several times to grasp the significance—and novelty—of the definitions Arendt offers, each of which both captures a basic experience and shows how the terms that have been used to define it in the past have obscured that experience. This is not a field manual to help us identify an enemy, as *The Origins of Totalitarianism* is; it is a primer on how to think about and evaluate the *res publica,* the public things; how to protect them once they've been identified; and how to live a political life. The same vision guides the accompanying case study, *On Revolution,* which discusses the American revolutionary spirit and the ideal of republicanism.

After a brief prologue, Arendt offers three pages in which the definitions crucial to the whole of *The Human Condition* are announced trenchantly, without a word said about where these definitions had come from or why they were so crucial to her reading of human history. A whole worldview—a revolutionary one—is compressed into the pages in which she declares that three activities are fundamental for humans: labor, work, and action. Each corresponds to a universal and basic condition "under which life on earth has been given to man."[3] (Of course "on earth" has always seemed a basic human condition, unchallenged until the present era of space travel, which potentially offers people a way to escape the condition of living on Earth.)

"The human condition of labor is life itself." That is, people must labor to supply themselves with the necessities of food and safety that sustain life. "The human condition of work is world-liness." In their natural, earthly surroundings, people must build a "world," whether of portable shelters, farms, settlements, villages, city-states, empires, or nations, which they can inhabit and cultivate, developing *cultura.* "Plurality is the condition of human action." No two human beings are alike, so people must relate to one another, must come together, find ways to live together, negotiate their differences, exchange opinions, found relational political institutions in the world they have created. A person may labor alone or be a fabricator alone, but "action is completely dependent upon the constant presence of others." Among the animals, a human being, as Aristotle said, is uniquely a *zoon politikon,* a creature of political relations. There are other conditions, too, including the temporally defining conditions of human existence, natality and mortality: a person must be born and must die. Arendt notes that action also has a close connection to the condition of natality because "the new beginning inherent in birth can make itself felt in the world only because the newcomer possesses the capacity of beginning something anew, that is, of acting."[4]

Western history, when examined through the lens of this cascade of definitions, is a saga in which the three basic activities have been differently experienced and differently thought about and evaluated at different times. The ancient Greeks of the post-Homeric Classical Age gave little praise to labor and work because, in their evaluation, these activities simply supplied necessities. Their admiration and attention were reserved for action (public words and deeds), which moves beyond necessities; it is free (that is, it is not needed to supply necessities) and engaged in by free men, not laborers (including slaves) or artisans (or even artists), although workers do have the culture-creating responsibility of memorializing action. So Aristotle, when he considered the different ways people live their lives, looked only to the ways *free* men live—seeking pleasure, acting, and thinking (the highest way). (As "the highest and perhaps purest activity," thinking is not considered by Arendt a fundamental condition for humans, for it is not open to all.)[5] Of these modes of free living, Plato treasured only thinking, and that evaluation of the various activities has had a decisive influence on Western philosophy. After the ancient Greek and Roman city-states disappeared, action became less esteemed; it fell into the realm of necessities along with labor and work, so that the only truly free activity, it seemed to the Platonically influenced Christian philosophers, was thinking, which meant contemplating the divine. To the Christian contemplatives, the source of all truth was found not in the people and things of this world revealing themselves but in the transcendent Word of God, which could be heard only by withdrawing into the chamber of the solitary thinking self.

Ever since Plato, Arendt claimed, those dedicated to contemplation have looked down on labor, work, and action, and from their lofty, prejudiced vantage point they have misunderstood all three. Their contempt for laborers, workers, and actors, or more generally contemptus mundi, is the very opposite of Arendt's amor mundi. Arendt expressed this opinion many times, but never more succinctly than in a footnote to *On Revolution* that defined the position she herself occupied, between the past that valued philosophy and the future she hoped for in which political action would be appreciated: "The hostility between philosophy and politics, barely covered up by a philosophy of politics, has been the curse of Western statecraft as well as of the Western tradition of philosophy ever since the men of action and the men of thought parted company—that is, ever since Socrates' death."[6]

The key mental condition that makes it difficult for thoughtful modern Western people—even secularists—to face the realities of their world, to think what they are doing, is that they are heirs to the great prejudice of the Western Platonic philosophical tradition, particularly held by its Christian contributors. When the contemplative life is privileged over the active life (the *vita activa*), action is especially distrusted. Contemplatives want to control or eliminate the uncontrolled, unpredictable realm of action and speech, the political realm. Under the influence of this prejudice, the word *politics,* which for Arendt refers to human beings acting—discoursing, persuading, deciding on specific deeds, doing them—in the public realm, came to refer to the rulership of one or more human beings over others. Politics equals government. In almost the entire Western political tradition, she held, it has been assumed that "the essence of politics is rulership and that the dominant political passion is the passion to rule or to govern."[7] Even the majority of revolutionaries, determined to overthrow rulers, do not imagine that they are making way for action, releasing action, as it were, from bondage; they want only to impose a different kind of rulership.

Arendt's point, crucial to her effort to understand how human freedom is experienced and can be preserved, is that there are two fundamental types of thinking about politics, of defining politics. On the one hand, you can think of politics as government, domination of some people (one or a few or many) over other people, requiring the threat or use of violence. Or, on the other hand you can think of politics, as she did, as the organization or constitution of the power people have when they come together as talking and acting beings. Here her emphasis is on preserving the people's power in a constituted government: *potestas in populo.*

Most heirs of the Western contemplative tradition's prejudice against action are not, of course, contemplatives. Arendt argued that the prejudice against action became common even among actors—even among revolutionaries, especially those well versed in the political theories wherein the prejudice is taken for granted. *On Revolution,* as an illustration of *The Human Condition,* explores why revolutionaries typically turn against the unpredictable situations they find themselves in or bring about, and why they try to make those situations—craft them, fabricate them—into something more controllable. They search for an authority to replace the authority rebelled against and for a mechanism to permanently make the distribution of the fruits of labor, the necessities of life, more equitable. In so doing, they come to focus on purposes from the domains of labor and work, rather than action. And with that misfocus they lose what the American revolutionaries, living in a land with far less poverty and social injustice than pre-revolutionary France or Russia, tried to maintain in their constitution—uniquely, in Arendt's view: the "public happiness" of acting and talking.

Among modern intellectuals, the prejudice against action is commonly held by those who have retreated from the world for purposes other than contemplation and who desire separation from others not in solitude (which they may equate with loneliness) but in some kind of individual or group distinction (an extreme individualism or elitism), which is either self-designated or determined by the prevailing mode of celebrity. As I noted, in her youth Arendt was fiercely critical of the Romantics for their preoccupation with crafting or fabricating themselves, making themselves into works of art. In conversation she was equally critical of people who went in for psychoanalysis, which she also viewed (wrongly, I think) as a kind of assisted self-crafting. If she were alive today, I imagine that she would focus her critique on people who impose their self-image on other people, demanding acknowledgment, reward, or fame. Her fear was that self-preoccupation in any form would lead to the modern version of contemptus mundi, which she called world-alienation, if it did not spring from world-alienation in the first place. And self-preoccupied, world-alienated people cannot appreciate the public realm where action takes place.

Arendt's admiration of Jaspers centered on her judgment that he was completely unusual for a modern philosopher: he did not distrust the public realm, despite his experience with Nazism.

"Jaspers's affirmation of the public realm is unique because it comes from a philosopher and because it springs from the fundamental conviction underlying his whole activity as a philosopher: that both philosophy and politics concern everyone. This is what they have in common; this is the reason they belong in the public realm where the human person and his ability to prove himself are what count. The philosopher—in contrast to the scientist—resembles the statesman in that he must answer for his opinions, that he is held responsible. The statesman, in fact, is in the relatively fortunate position of being responsible only to his own nation, whereas Jaspers, at least in all of his writings after 1933, has always written as if to answer for himself before all of mankind."[8]

With Jaspers's example in mind Arendt offered a philosophical analysis of action that she thought would present it without the usual philosophical prejudice. She began where he did, with the idea that action is open to all people, in all their diversity or plurality; it requires no special talents (although in many situations it requires the virtue of courage) because it arises from ("is ontologically rooted in") the human condition of natality, the condition of being born. So action is initiation, characterized by its unexpectedness or novelty, its unpredictability. As a beginning or an initiation, action reveals *who* a person is, as distinct from every other person but related to all, related, potentially, to all humankind.

Acting persons reveal their self or, really, it would be more concrete to say reveal their self in relation to others, with whom and for whom the doing or talking (the acting) is performed. The founding fathers putting pen to paper and announcing, "We hold these truths to be self-evident . . ." might stand as model actors in Arendt's terms. So action is quite different from behavior, which is repetitive and habitual, showing what people have become, not who they can become in the performance of action, which forces them to rise to an occasion. Arendt thought that behavior could be judged by moral criteria as right or wrong; but action is judged for neither its motivation nor its aim, only its performance, and the only criterion for judging an action is greatness.[9] (In *The Human Condition*, Arendt declared that greatness is the one criterion for judging action without engaging the obvious political and moral question of whether there are good and bad actions, good and bad greatness; but she returned to the issue in *The Life of the Mind*.)

Action is intimately bound to mortality, too. Human beings make works that they hope will be immortal and thereby address the inevitability of mortality, but the human deeds and words that artists and storytellers present and hand down from generation to generation are what really address that mortality. In action, people win glory or renown, "immortal fame."

In her section on action, Arendt described what action means to and does for actors: it reveals who they are, and it is as those revealed actors that they become the subjects of stories. But she concentrated upon the frustrations or hazards action poses to human beings because it is the calamities of action ("the frailty of human affairs") that have, throughout the Western tradition, made thinkers and often actors as well hostile to it and have prompted the various efforts to eliminate or control it. The chief hazard of action is that it has effects that are uncontrollable, unstoppable, and unpredictable. The chief frustration is that, unlike fabrications, which are products of work, actions cannot be named or compassed in words as they are unfolding; they can be named and understood only when they have ended—often a long time after they have ended. It was her opinion, for example, that for thirty years after the First World War no work of art appeared that "transparently displayed the inner truth of the event," although there were shelves of descriptions; but then William Faulkner's novel *A Fable*, with its "tragic effect," was able to help its readers "accept the fact that something like this war could have happened at all," to face its reality.[10]

This frustration of action can be described from another angle by saying that actions do not have results the way fabricating processes do; an actor's actions become part of a web of other people's actions, and such a web, never still and solid, cannot be understood or viewed as a whole until the actors have exited the stage. Human beings, when they act, "know not what they do" in the sense that they do not know the consequences of their actions, for themselves or for others. Arendt saw the genre of tragedy (whether in the theater or fiction) as particularly illuminating because it represents "a process of recognition": "The tragic hero becomes knowledgeable by re-experiencing what has been done in the way of suffering, and in this *pathos,* in resuffering the past, the network of individual acts is transformed into an event, a significant whole." But her point about storytelling was also more general: "In contradistinction to other elements peculiar to action—above all to the preconceived goals, the compelling motives, and the guiding principles, all of which become visible in the course of action—the meaning of a committed act is revealed only when the action itself has come to an end and become a story susceptible to narration."[11]

When people try to imagine acting as though it were a kind of fabrication, attempting to determine its story in advance, they are governed by visions of ends to be achieved and means to those ends. They have conceptualized action in terms of work, and they rationalize their deeds with sayings like "you can't make an omelet without breaking eggs" or "the end justifies the means." In *On Revolution,* Arendt astutely noted that in the modern world both revolutionaries, often following Marx, and counterrevolutionaries, people dedicated to preventing revolutions, have assumed that violence is *necessary* to politics, as chiseling is necessary to stone sculpture, and this is because they think of action as a kind of fabrication: it "makes history." Because action, unlike a fabrication, is unpredictable, it requires not skill or strength or application of violent force for achieving a result, but courage in the face of the unknown; action is risk.

Arendt held that the pre-Platonic Greeks, the first theorists of action, understood that action depends not on organized or legislatively created spaces for action, or on political organization or government, but simply on people coming together to share words and deeds: "the unreliable and only temporary agreement of many wills and intentions."[12] This coming together of actors is what Arendt called power, and she distinguished power sharply both from individual strength (self-sufficiency) and from instrumental violence or force. Unlike most political theorists and unlike most revolutionaries or counterrevolutionaries, Arendt did not think of power as dependent upon the possession of means of violence; on the contrary, she held that people resort to violence when they do not have or have lost power.

My friend Jerome Kohn and I have often remarked to each other that of all Arendt's many distinctions, each of which requires of her readers a willingness to undergo a revolution in thought, her distinction between power and violence is perhaps the most challenging.[13] She was really arguing that power and violence are *opposites*. Hers was not an argument like Gandhi's for nonviolence, but an argument for power, which is most powerful when it is nonviolent. Particularly for people like us, who live in a world where it is routinely assumed that those with the biggest armies or arsenals, or the ultimate weapon, are the ones with power—or even "superpower"—and where it is assumed that power means the capacity to rule over others, her distinction is hard to understand and its implications hard to imagine. And it certainly makes no sense to those who believe that a display of violence is the way to assert power, which is the basic premise, to give a current illustration, of the U.S. government's strategic document published in 1996, "Shock and Awe: Achieving Rapid Dominance," the blueprint developed after the First Gulf War and resurrected for the current American military operation in Iraq. This paper asserts that if a government uses violence ("shock and awe") to destroy "the will to resist before, during and after battle" and to create a "feeling of impotence," the enemy will collapse.[14] But the example of many years of bombardment of Vietnam, or the more recent examples of the bombardments of Afghanistan and Iraq, should have taught anyone with eyes to see that, short of experiencing Hiroshima-like devastation, the people of a bombarded nation (particularly one bombarded preemptively) will retreat but then regroup for further action, generating power. Not a feeling of impotence, but a will to join others in resistance—an empowerment—will drive them.

The distinction between power and violence is particularly hard to appreciate when violence has already been resorted to, that is, in wars, which under contemporary technological conditions will be "won" by those with superior means of violence. Such a "victory" further persuades people that violence is power. But under contemporary conditions such a victory really means that the victor resorted to violence from lack of power, that it was unwilling or unable to find a nonviolent way to deal with its enemies: by lining up a solid rank of allies, by appealing to dissenters within the enemy camp, by diplomacy and influence upon world opinion, by bringing offenders before an international tribunal, and so forth. A military victory, furthermore, is no guarantee that peace will not prove a prelude to further war when the defeated group has regrouped, which is why the twentieth-century invention of "unconditional surrender" has become an aspiration to fabricate the impossible—that is, definitively end a war without the nonviolent action of mutual promises or treaty making to bind the combatants. In Arendt's terms, the power most likely to be lasting, the one that can best preserve the actors' humanity, is the power that arises from nonviolent action. For nonviolent action requires speech; it involves continuing discussion and a respectful exchange of opinions, which are a means of renewing power. "Binding and promising, combining and covenanting are the means by which power is kept in existence."[15]

Arendt's faith in the power of the people rests on a conviction that people fundamentally desire the "public happiness" that comes from acting in concert, bonding together for their common good. Among Western political philosophers, the one who most clearly held the opposite conviction was the Englishman Thomas Hobbes, author of *Leviathan,* whose sound bite on the human condition is that it is "war of all against all." Since its publication in 1651, Hobbes's book has found fans in every generation, but among its current followers are many who do not spend their lives in the library. A cadre of neoconservatives in Washington read *Leviathan* under the guidance of Leo Strauss, an émigré contemporary of Arendt's, who in his years at the University of Chicago developed out of his *Philosophy of Thomas Hobbes* (1936) and his many later admiring studies of Plato's writings about philosopher-kings a conservative program he thought essential for the modern world.[16] (One of Strauss's Bush administration disciples, Paul Wolfowitz, appears in his hawkish "Leocon" guise as a character in the Chicago-based novelist Saul Bellow's *Ravelstein.*)

Strauss, fiercely critical of the decadence and incivility of the modern world, and dedicated to sponsoring an elite of kingly philosophers to cure these ills, had recognized in Hobbes a man whose lack of faith in people and lack of hope for action matched his own. Hobbes had started reasoning from the premise that in terms of violence all men are terrifyingly equal, for "the weakest has strength enough to kill the strongest, either by secret machination, or by confederacy with others, that are in the same danger with himself." Since they live in "continual fear, and danger of violent death," men in their natural state "have no pleasure, but on the contrary a great deal of grief, in keeping company."[17] So, Hobbes concluded, a sovereign state must relieve them of their terror. Strauss added to this logic that the state must also lie to the people—tell Platonic "noble lies"—in the service of security.

Assuming that fear of violent death, rather than the desire to keep company with others, is the basic human motivation Hobbes envisioned a state that would ensure control over potential conspirators, revolutionaries, or any people whatsoever who acted together. Hobbes's Leviathan, his commonwealth, is an "artificial man," a "mortal God," that "overawes" its subjects; they forfeit to the state all rights except the "natural" right to preserve their individual lives by any means in the case of war with other states. What Hobbes called "mixed government" or "diversity of opinions"—precisely what Arendt believed gave rise to power—could only weaken the "absolute power" of Leviathan, an artifact made by men who desire its stability so that they can be left to pursue their private, mainly economic, interests. The "absolute" or "sovereign" power of Hobbes's commonwealth means that justice and law are simply what it decrees them to be. With his relentless logic Hobbes does not shy away from the fact that Leviathan is a tyranny, for "tyranny, signifieth nothing more, nor less, than the name of sovereignty." The only downside to the Hobbesian sovereign state is that the people, who have signed over their freedom in exchange for state protection, must help the state protect itself. They must send their sons into its army, for Leviathan will "live in the condition of perpetual war, and upon the confines of battle, with [its] frontiers armed, and cannons planted against [its] neighbors round about."[18] But Hobbes thought perpetual war was a price worth paying for domestic security—or what we would now call "homeland security."

Ultimately, it seems to me, a bleak, misanthropic vision like Hobbes's stands behind every justification (including the ideological totalitarian ones) for perpetual state violence or what Hobbes called state power. The vision is of complete fusion of power and violence. And the idea is that Leviathan will shock and awe not only all external enemies in the perpetual war that Hobbes accepted as natural; it will keep its own citizens in a state of awe at its power and violence: they will find it "the mightiest nation on earth." When a republic, a mixed government, goes over to this vision, it is headed for tyranny rationalized as sovereignty. From Arendt's point of view there could be no clearer signal of a crisis of the republic than the espousal of such a vision by government officials—so the current espousal of it among the Straussian neo-conservatives in Washington is not something to be taken lightly. Not even the ex-Communist ideologues of the McCarthy period went so far in their rationalization for silencing dissent and preparing for perpetual war.

Action is threatened when people do not understand the way it generates power, having confused power with violence and the assertion of sovereignty through different forms of government. But Arendt also thought that under modern, post-totalitarian conditions particular forms of government, which reflected particular traditional biases against "the diversity of opinion" and action, offered only one threat to action. Society itself, with its depersonalizing modes, its mechanization and commodification, its promotion of social conformism and thoughtlessness, offered an equal threat. In a 1954 lecture, she made the double focus of her concern for action clear: "The world's central problems today are the political organization of mass societies and the political integration of technical power."[19]

I shall return to Arendt's reflections on the political integration of technology, but let me give an example here of what her concern implied for action. She held that modern battlefields permit no revelations of who an actor is, no deeds to be judged great; rather, they are like meetings of speechless robots, some of whom kill and some of whom are killed. Saturation and nuclear bombing were the totalitarian degree of the same depersonalization phenomenon, a development that, obviously, lives on as a totalitarian legacy in nontotalitarian states and that has, more recently, been appropriated as a threat from and a practice of nonstate groups of terrorists. Suicide bombers could be described in her terms as those who do not reveal their *who* more thoroughly than any type of modern soldier. The suicide bomber is purely an instrument of violence—a bomb—programmed for self-destruction and the destruction of others; such people resemble pilotless drones, the kind of completely depersonalized shock-and-awe bombardier used by nations.

The characteristics of action that I have summarized are key for understanding what Arendt had to say about making promises and forgiveness, the two forms of action that most deeply address the uncertainty and risk of action in general—and that are the strongest counters to the repressive Hobbesian Leviathan. In the brief, dense pages at the end of her discussion of action in which she considers promising and forgiving, Arendt anticipated, I think, how these two domains of political life would be reevaluated in the post-totalitarian world, not just philosophically, but politically, in action. And this anticipation of hers, I also think, is the crucial aspect to elaborate on when we ask what her understanding of action can offer us now, when both forums for forgiveness and forums for making promises have appeared in unprecedented ways in councils and conventions.

Again, she began with definitions. Forgiveness is the human faculty for undoing—reversing—deeds and words that have been done and spoken. Or, to cite another formulation, forgiveness is "the necessary corrective for the inevitable damages resulting from action." As a potentiality of action itself, forgiveness arises out of action to address "the predicament of irreversibility" in action, that is, the predicament of being "unable to undo what one has done though one did not, and could not, have known what he was doing."[20] Forgiveness addresses the boundless happenings of the past, while the human capacity to make and keep promises (or contracts or treaties) addresses the unpredictability of action, thereby providing some degree of security.

Readers who do not understand that Arendt has ruled many phenomena out of her consideration because they are not action in her sense will find her reflections on the action of forgiveness baffling. For example, forgiveness for Arendt does not relate to behavior, that is, to those repetitive daily behaviors which are judged by moral criteria or moral rules as right or wrong, rather than by the criterion of greatness. Judging a deed wrong is not the first step toward forgiving it; indeed, in Arendt's view one does not forgive a deed at all, but the doer of a deed, a person. One person says to another not "This deed is wrong" (as would be the case in a courtroom) but "*You* have harmed me," or "*You* have harmed these people, by doing what you have done." Forgiveness does not relate directly to what has been done and does not belong to the moral domain that most discussions of forgiveness focus upon. In Arendt's conception, forgiveness, as an action, is a type of relationship, an expression of the human condition of plurality.

In another way, too, forgiveness is not of the moral domain as traditionally—that is, Platonically—conceived. In the philosophical tradition, so hostile to action, morality is thought to flow out from a well-ordered ruler or ruling group into the world. Plato's vision of a philosopher-king was also an effort to imagine political rulership as legitimated by rulership over the self: as a ruler rules himself, so he rules over others. For those who think this way, a well-ordered public realm seems to be a kind of projection outward of a person who is a morally correct work of art. But for the faculties of forgiving and promising a completely different set of guiding principles is involved, because the domain of action is the domain of plurality: experiences with others, not inside the self, determine the moral ambiance for forgiving and promising. On the basis of relationships with others, the self becomes able to have internal forgiving and promising relations between "me and myself."

The Platonic moral code flows from the self outward to others, while, as Arendt put it: "the extent and modes of being for-given and being promised determine the extent and modes in which one may be able to forgive himself or keep promises con-cerned only with himself."[21] Self-forgiveness presumes the ways in which forgiveness operates between people, its proper domain. At one point, Arendt goes so far as to argue that self-forgiveness is not possible because forgiveness requires that another see who you are—and you cannot see who you are yourself. (And this is, by the way, a very psychoanalytic idea.)

Further, Arendt's conception of forgiveness most importantly does not relate to what she called "the extremities of crimes and willed evil," that is, to exactly those human deeds that are (rightly, in my estimation) considered the most challenging to almost all contemporary theorists of forgiveness. Arendt preferred to use "to trespass" for the speaking and doing that can be forgiven because this verb, which translates *hamartanein* in ancient and New Tes-tament Greek, means "to miss the mark" or go astray, as an arrow misses a target, not to commit a crime or intend to do harm or do evil. She thought that a person who goes astray, who tres-passes, differed from one who knowingly commits "offences," the noun Arendt uses to translate the New Testament Greek noun *skandala*.[22]

This biblical verb "to trespass" brings us to the crucial matter to bear in mind while considering Arendt's reflections on forgive-ness. Her touchstone for conceptualizing action was the writings of the pre-Platonic Greek poets, historians, and dramatists in which action was so appreciated, but her touchstone for reflect-ing on forgiveness was the New Testament Gospels containing the sayings of Jesus of Nazareth, a thinker living in a historical period characterized by suspicion of words and deeds and a strong unworldliness. Her pages on "the power to forgive" are, in effect, indebted for their conceptualization to a thinker, Jesus, who deeply appreciated the hazards and calamities of action, while the pages defining action generally are indebted to the Greek experience of the glories of action.

One might, to consider more concretely what the European tradition had to offer Arendt and what it has to offer us, call to mind the beautiful scene that ends Homer's *Iliad*. Priam, king of Troy, has come to the tent of Achilles to beg for the return of his defeated son Hector's body, which Achilles has been abusing by dragging it around all day behind his chariot—a terrible trespass against the rules of war. The old Trojan king and the most glorious of the young Achaean warriors admire each other. Achilles, touched, remembering his own father, relents and offers Priam hospitality. No forgiveness for abusing Hector's body is asked for or given. The poem ends with this moment of exquisite stillness and equipoise, but every Greek who listened to it knew—as we modern readers do, too—that the next day Achilles would return to battle and, before he died, help plan the sack of Troy, in which Priam would also die, along with Hector's son, and his widow would be taken into slavery. The moment of stillness had no power of reversal.

In *The Human Condition*, Arendt noted that Jesus spoke as a religious leader, but his thinking, because it relates to a fundamental human experience, was political and of great political significance. That Jesus' concept of forgiveness was primarily political, reflecting the experience of a "small and closely knit community" challenging the Roman public authorities, she argues, is attested to by the fact that Jesus taught that forgiveness must be practiced among people before they can hope to be forgiven by God. Forgiveness is necessary because people "know not what they do: that is, their ordinary daily doings need forgiving, or dismissing, in order to make it possible for life to go on by constantly releasing men from what they have done unknowingly." As we will see later, this word *releasing* is much better for her purposes than *undoing* or *reversing* for it carries no implication that the deed is forgotten or dissolved in some way, while *releasing* implies being unbound from the past in order to go on; it is a letting go. "Only through this constant mutual release from what they do can men remain free agents, only by constant willingness to change their minds and start again can they be trusted with so great power as that to begin something new."[23] The emphasis is on *mutual* release.

On the other hand, when people *knowingly* do evil and commit crimes, they will be taken care of not by other people but by God, at the Last Judgment, when God deals out not forgiveness but retribution. In Luke 17:1-5, Jesus speaks of *skandala* (offences), which are unforgivable on earth. For one who offends unforgivably "it would be better that a millstone were hanged around his neck, and he cast into the sea."

In these passages, it seems clear that Arendt thought that Jesus considered a person an unforgivable offender for presuming (like a fabricator "making history") to know the consequences of an action and, further, for acting knowingly, with conscious intention, to do harm—with conscious intention to murder, for example. In what she wrote, it is not clear whether she herself thought a person who knowingly committed an offence (such as a murderer) should ever be forgiven or whether the offender should be left to God's judgment and retribution. What is clear is that she did not use the words *forgivable* and *unforgivable* about offences, only about actors: for actions, her terms were *punishable* and *unpunishable*. She noted that the only alternative to forgiveness for stopping or stepping out of the irreversibility and boundlessness of action is punishment, which is, in this respect, very different from taking vengeance. Vengeance reenacts the original trespass or offence, perpetuating the cycle of damage or calamity, without in any way releasing the parties from it.

In her brief discussion of punishment, Arendt does not return to the distinction between a trespasser and an offender. She does not consider the question of whether, by her definition, trespassers are punishable and offenders not. If she had claimed that offenders were unpunishable she would, of course, have come into conflict with the provisions of most modern legal codes, which do list punishments for premeditated crimes; those who have merely trespassed are not the only inhabitants of prisons. Arendt did not see the problem in her formulation, I think, because she was hurrying ahead toward the general formulation that it is "a structural element in the realm of human affairs, that men are unable to forgive what they cannot punish and that they are unable to punish what has turned out to be unforgivable." In this formulation, it is obvious that she was really thinking of totalitarian crimes against humanity, not just crimes like murder, for she repeats the formulation in her comment that unpunishability and unforgivability together are "the true hallmark of those offenses which, since Kant, we call 'radical evil,' and about whose nature so little is known, even to us who have been exposed to one of their rare outbursts [that is, the Nazi crimes] on the public scene. All we know is that we can neither punish nor forgive such offenses and that they thus transcend the realm of human affairs and the potentialities of human power, both of which they radically destroy wherever they make their appearance."[24]

Written before her book on Eichmann, these remarks, which are categorical about the unforgivability of radical evil, also leave unexplored the actors—offenders—who are neither trespassers (both forgivable and punishable) nor doers of radical evil (both unforgivable and unpunishable). Further, they leave unexplored what, if any, conditions the person who is forgiven must meet to merit forgiveness. In this connection, Arendt does cite Luke 17:4: "And if he trespass against thee seven times a day, and seven times in a day turn again to thee, saying, I repent, thou shalt forgive him." The verb translated "repent" in this passage is *metanoein,* which literally means "to change one's mind," so the person who is forgiven must offer or reveal this change of mind or repentance. But Arendt does not say whether she thinks that changing one's mind merits forgiveness only for trespassers or whether those who have committed offences can, if they change their minds, merit forgiveness as well. This is precisely the challenging territory explored in the contemporary political innovation pioneered twenty years after Arendt's death in South Africa, the Truth and Reconciliation Commission.

And it is just as significant that neither Jesus nor Arendt in her commentary says anything further about what the change of mind that qualifies a person for forgiveness consists of. Is it a change from not knowing what one is doing to knowing what one has done? Or from not knowing the consequences of a deed and then, when the consequences become knowable, regretting the action? Feeling remorse? Does the change of mind require only a declaration? Or does it demand insight into the harm caused, empathy for those harmed? Does it necessitate a counter-deed, an offer of reparations or an offer to accept some form of punishment? Does it entail a promise not to do the harmful deed again? I am not posing these questions with the idea that there is or should be a code governing qualification for forgiveness, but rather because when people do try to decide whether to forgive someone or whether someone is forgivable, they usually expect that person to show repentance and, further, they come to a sense (more or less articulated) of what that repentance should involve (unless the person to be forgiven has died and can no longer offer repentance). Often it is the case, too, that the one who forgives also has a kind of change of mind, giving up an initial desire for vengeance or an unwillingness to forgive. Putting questions of this sort is often part of a forgiving person's change of mind and process of reaching a judgment to forgive.

The silence in all of Jesus' formulations (including the well-known parable of the Prodigal Son) about what a trespasser's change of mind should consist of was the root, I think, of the development within the Christian religion and church of the rituals of confession and absolution, or reinstatement in the community. These are rituals of conditional forgiveness, requiring confession of fault and submission to punishment. Contrition is followed by absolution, absolution by penance. Unconditional forgiveness is very rare, and it may presume the unconditional love shown in the Prodigal Son parable by the father: "He was lost, and is found" is all the forgiving father says. However, as we can learn from the experiences of the Truth and Reconciliation Commission, some people do feel that a perpetrator who does not repent can be forgiven on the principle that a higher social good of peace and reconciliation is served by forgiveness.

In only one passage in her discussion of forgiveness does Arendt link the psychological condition of the forgiving person to the psychological condition of a repentant person who is forgiven. After she observes that forgiving shows the same revelatory character as the deed forgiven, in the sense that it is the person who did the deed who is forgiven, not what was done, and it is a person who forgives, she notes that Jesus had made this who/what distinction in a very specific way by saying such things as: "Her sins, which are many, are forgiven; for she loved much: but to whom little is forgiven, the same loveth little." Arendt remarks that this implicit criterion—that forgiveness should be bestowed on those who are revealed as loving (nothing is said here about repentance)—has led to "the current conviction that only love has the power to forgive," which she thought was not the case. Love does, she says, have "an unequaled power of self-revelation and an unequaled clarity for the disclosure of *who,* precisely because it is unconcerned to the point of total unworldliness with what the loved person may be, with his qualities and shortcomings no less than with his achievements, failings and transgressions." But love is very rare and forgiveness is constantly needed to repair the web of human action. So she describes another relational quality in the forgiving person (and, implicitly, in the political milieu) that can support forgiveness:

> If it were true, therefore, as Christianity assumed, that only love can forgive because only love is fully receptive to who somebody is, to the point of being always willing to forgive him no matter what he may have done, forgiving would have to remain altogether outside our considerations. Yet what love is in its own narrowly circumscribed sphere, respect is in the larger domain of human affairs. Respect, not unlike the Aristotelian *philia politike,* is a kind of "friendship" without intimacy and without closeness; it is a regard for the person from the distance which the space of the world puts between us. . . . Thus the modern loss of respect, or rather the conviction that respect is due only where we admire or esteem, constitutes a clear symptom of the increasing depersonalization of public and social life.[25]

So Arendt, in effect, ruled out of her political consideration unconditional forgiveness (which might relate to either trespassers or offenders) and the unconditional love on which it is based as phenomena too rare to have political meaning or political implications. Her call to appreciate respect is, it seems to me, vitally important, but I also think that her ruling out of political consideration unconditional forgiveness perhaps does not enough appreciate the influence of those few individuals capable of the *imitatio Christi* that the Christian religion extols and demands of its faithful (provoking thereby an enormous amount of guilt among those who fall short of the ideal and an enormous amount of hypocrisy among those who pretend to have achieved the ideal).

Later, when she wrote a reflection on Pope John XXIII at the time of his death, Arendt seemed to be much more aware that a man who took the challenge of imitatio Christi seriously and organized his life around it could have enormous political importance: "The Christian on St. Peter's Chair," as she called him, led a revolution in the Catholic Church which the church hierarchy has been trying to stop and roll back ever since.[26] His actions, certainly worthy of the judgment "great," revealed him as a person. And the example of John XXIII certainly had its impact upon his successor, the Polish-born John Paul II, who, even though he was a rigidly conservative supporter of church hierarchy and formulated policies that have had devastating consequences for the impoverished Catholic populations most ravaged by unsustainable birthrates and sexually transmitted diseases, was a proponent of forgiveness. On a personal level, he offered forgiveness to his would-be assassin. More important politically, it was he who made a journey to Jerusalem to ask forgiveness of a representative group of Jewish leaders for the silence of the wartime pope and church.

Both John XXIII and John Paul II had a great influence on the rise at the end of the twentieth century, after Arendt's death, of real political interest in forgiveness, although neither put forgiveness at the center of his political actions as strongly as His Holiness the Dalai Lama. The Dalai Lama even displays generous concern for the Chinese people, whose national army has been brutally occupying Tibet for more than fifty years. In his 1989 Nobel Peace Prize acceptance speech, he acknowledged that the Chinese people had been deeply damaged by their own Cultural

Revolution, during which their government perpetrated the murder of one-sixth of the Tibetan population and began the destruction of Tibet's religious and cultural heritage. The Dalai Lama has repeatedly offered the promise of his Five Point Peace Plan to successive Chinese governments and called for dialogue and negotiations—to no avail, as yet.

When Arendt wrote about Pope John XXIII, a man whose grace under pressure during the controversies set off by his democratizing policies was extraordinary, she had just begun the ordeal of her own controversy, over the publication of *Eichmann in Jerusalem*. There, as I have indicated, she took up again the topic of radical evil, about which she had now changed her mind. We need to reconsider this story in the context of forgiveness.

In *The Origins of Totalitarianism*, Arendt had written about the ideologies but never the individual motives of the Nazis, although she had assumed they had motives. These criminal motives—intentions to do harm—were deeply rooted, radical, to the point of being incomprehensible, or being conjurable only by means of references to the devil or assumptions of innate murderous aggression or original sin. After listening to Eichmann at his trial and reading the pretrial interviews with him, she concluded that he had no criminal motives but only motives—not criminal in themselves—related to his own advancement in the Nazi hierarchy. He was neither a man who did not know what he was doing nor a man who intended to do harm; he was a man who, conforming to the prevailing norms and his Führer's will, failed altogether to grasp the meaning of what he was doing. He was not diabolical, he was thoughtless, which is (as I have noted) the word Arendt used for a mental condition reflecting remoteness from reality, inability to grasp a reality that stares you in the face—a failure of imagination and judgment. She commented: "That such remoteness from reality and thoughtlessness can wreck more havoc than all the evil instincts taken together which, perhaps, are inherent in man—that was, in fact, the lesson one could learn in Jerusalem."[27] No deep-rooted or radical evil was necessary to make the trains to Auschwitz run on time.

Arendt did not assume that Eichmann's mental condition was the condition of all Nazis (she remained silent about Hitler himself and about Himmler, in order to avoid reducing the problem of totalitarian evil to a problem of evil leadership). And she certainly did not assume, as some commentators on her book alleged, that there is an Eichmann in everyone; an assumption of a kind of negative solidarity as innate as that supposed by the doctrine of original sin. Further, she did not think that Eichmann merited forgiveness for his assertions to the court that he had neither acted from base motives nor intended to kill anybody. Although he acknowledged that the Nazi policies were considered criminal by others, Eichmann did not think of himself as a criminal because he had only done what his Führer ordered him to do and what the laws of the land called for. Like the Nazis on trial after the war in Nuremburg, he showed no remorse or repentance.

In Arendt's view, forgiveness for Eichmann was not a possibility, and no reflection on how incommensurate any punishment would be to his crime should have kept the court in Jerusalem from the demonstration that she thought it had rightly made by sentencing Eichmann to death: namely, a demonstration (so Arendt put it in her own words) that Eichmann, by carrying out a state policy of mass murder aimed at eliminating the Jewish people and others from the earth, deserved that no member of the human race would want to share the earth with him. By phrasing the court's message in these terms, Arendt made it clear that she thought that Eichmann, a new form of criminal acting as the agent of a criminal state, by carrying out this new form of crime against humanity, had violated the whole order of the international community. Implicitly, she was also saying that he had violated as well the fundamental order of the human condition, of human life as it is lived on earth. Human life is lived in the world, with diverse others, all of whom are able to begin anew (and must not be deprived of this capacity), and all of whom will die (and must not be eliminated prematurely). As she argued, "These modern, state-employed mass murderers must be prosecuted because they violated the order of mankind, and not because they killed millions of people. Nothing is more pernicious to an understanding of these new crimes, or stands more in the way of the emergence of an international penal code that could take care of them, than the common illusion that the crime of murder and the crime of genocide are essentially the same, and that the latter therefore is 'no new crime properly speaking.' The point of the latter is that an altogether different order is broken and an altogether different community is violated."[28]

In Arendt's view, which Jaspers also argued, the most important dimension of the Eichmann trial politically, what distinguished it from the Nuremberg Trials and the various postwar successor trials, was the challenge it posed to the "emergence of an international penal code" that would accurately define the new crime, the unprecedented crime, that the midcentury totalitarian regimes had brought into the world. She anticipated that variations on crimes against humanity would appear in the future, particularly as technological developments like nuclear weapons and massive environmental pollutions made various kinds of state-sponsored genocide and ecocide more feasible. Although she did not think that the example of Eichmann's punishment would be a deterrent, she did think that the existence of an adequate international penal code would offer protection to people threatened with genocide or members of the species threatened with nuclear or biochemical disaster. The international community, responsible for protecting people against violations of "the order of mankind," needed to move beyond the Nuremberg precedents to legislation— and, it would be important to add from the perspective of the present, to *prevention* of crimes against humanity.

Directly and indirectly, Arendt's reflections on forgiveness have had great influence since 1958 when *The Human Condition* appeared, and that influence has increased since the 1980s, particularly as the Cold War ended and an international human rights community developed. Her chapter "The Power to Forgive" both helped initiate a discussion and reflected one that had already begun in the post-totalitarian world she was writing about.

Arendt had offered no contemporary examples of political forgiveness in her pages, perhaps because there had been so few to choose from during her lifetime. In the 1950s, her own words were, as all actions are, novel, a new beginning. There had been no precedent in modern political theory for reflections on forgiveness as a conditio sine qua non of politics, a fundamental political experience (not just a religious mandate), as there had been no precedent for drawing on the thought of Jesus of Nazareth as a historical person and political sage. Writing about Jesus as she did implied a rejection of the image being purveyed in the 1950s by theologians like Albert Schweitzer, who considered him the herald of the apocalypse and God's retribution for human sinfulness. This is the image that sustains the unforgiving, apocalyptic Christian fundamentalisms of today with their strictures about the straight and very narrow path that people must tread to be "born again," a needless qualification as all human beings already are new beginnings.

Arendt's reflections clarified the relation of forgiveness to politics: forgiveness is crucial to political existence, a fundamental experience for the person forgiven, for the forgiver, and for the political milieu in which their relationship evolves. Her reflections were thus ideally suited to the creation of a political theory that could be applied to the political practice of the American civil rights movement in the early 1960s. Martin Luther King, Jr., who also considered Jesus a political model, while Gandhi was his modern and directly political teacher, was developing, in his speeches throughout the 1960s up to his assassination in 1968, the basic conceptual chords that Arendt had sounded in *The Human Condition*. He noted, for example: "Forgiveness does not mean ignoring what has been done or putting a false label on an evil act.

It means, rather, that the evil act no longer remains as a barrier to the relationship."[29] Arendt's conceptualization of forgiveness as a necessary, generative ingredient of political life, a "*power*," not to be confused with absence of power, exoneration of or excuses for evil, or further victimization for those who take the path of forgiveness, has since become central to political discourse around the world under the broader, more political term *reconciliation*. But political actions are what have brought about this sea change that her conceptualization helped launch.

Most important, some fifteen years after Arendt's death in 1975, her ideas about forgiveness and her book on Eichmann influenced and were reflected in the action, the new beginning, that brought about the South African Truth and Reconciliation Commission (TRC), which, for the first time in history, made forgiveness a guiding principle for a state. The TRC was unprecedented, although forgiveness had been a guiding political principle at a more local level, in a few township and tribal community settings in countries like Uganda and Rwanda that provide forums for confronting perpetrators of crimes and giving them the opportunity to repent publicly. And now that the action of the Truth and Reconciliation Commission has concluded and some of its consequences can be seen, the time has come to tell the story of how forgiveness came into the public realm, in a way that goes beyond even Arendt's conceptualization.

The areas of Arendt's contribution that need to be considered in light of the South African experience are chiefly two, and those two are deeply connected: first, the relation of forgiveness to repentance and other qualifications for forgiveness, particularly for those Arendt called offenders, not trespassers; and second the relation of forgiveness to "extreme crimes and willed evil." I shall begin my exploration of these with the story of the TRC's work as told by the head of the commission, Archbishop Desmond Tutu, in his memoir *No Future Without Forgiveness*.

Let me recall as we turn to this text, that South Africa's last Afrikaner president, F. W. de Klerk, faced with the failure of his government's campaign for violent police suppression of the African National Congress (ANC) and other antiapartheid groups, had slowly come to realize in the late 1980s that the era of apartheid, which had formally begun in 1948, was coming to an end. He finally released the ANC's Nelson Mandela and other liberation fighters from prison and set up the Congress for a Democratic South Africa (CODESA), which organized the election that brought Mandela and his ANC party to power in 1994. President Mandela appointed the members of the Truth and Reconciliation Commission, which was charged with finding a way to break the cycle of state-administered violence that had gripped the country for nearly fifty years.

The members of the Truth and Reconciliation Commission clearly understood that the Nuremberg and Eichmann trials did not present a model for their work, because, as Tutu noted, the TRC had "to balance the requirements of justice, accountability, stability, peace, and reconciliation."[30] Reconciliation had had no role in the Nuremburg court, but it was perceived as necessary in South Africa. The Nazi leaders were tried by the non-German, Allied victors, not by fellow nationals who were still alive in majority numbers. Apartheid, "separateness," had not been a state policy for the elimination of nonwhite peoples, a Final Solution; it had been a protototalitarian state policy for depriving all non-white people of citizenship and relocating them away from areas designated for whites only. The policy extended to cover various kinds of discriminatory restrictions on education and economic development for nonwhites. In effect, it was a kind of enslavement, a continuation of the slave trade by other means.

After a violent police action in 1960 against unarmed, non-violent protesters that came to be known as the Sharpeville Massacre, a pattern of legislation to support police violence began. (The police were exonerated of any responsibility for the massacre.) Unlike in Germany, the police killings and tortures usually took place in designated remote centers or during cross-border raids and were directed against leaders of the antiapartheid movement. The goal was to establish absolute control over the nonwhites by killing their leaders and keeping them out of political life. It was not to destroy political life altogether, as was the case in the fully developed mid-twentieth-century totalitarian regimes. As apartheid came to an end, the black liberation fighters and their allies were faced with the task of finding a way to live in the same society with people who had wronged them so grievously, but they also had to deal with the criminal activities of the antiapartheid forces, which had become more and more violent as the government had clamped down on them.

The TRC was not a court. Its functions did not include sentencing or punishment; but it could issue amnesties both to people who had already faced judicial proceedings and to those who had not. It could not, however, offer a general amnesty of the sort engineered later by General Augusto Pinochet in Chile as a pre-condition to dissolving the junta he had led. That amnesty, which Pinochet arrogantly granted to himself, suppressed the truth, recognizing no *who,* no individual actors, and thus made a mockery of the Chilean Truth and Reconciliation Commission. In South Africa, people seeking amnesty had to make public statements and demonstrate that they had made a full disclosure of their actions; the burden of assembling evidence was on them, a requirement that brought out much more of the truth of what had happened than had the criminal trials conducted as apartheid ended (and while Afrikaners still dominated the courts). When the amnesty applications and documentation had been assembled, the TRC arranged meetings between perpetrators and their victims, people who had been tortured or who lost family members and comrades either to the state policy of killing and torture or to the antiapartheid resistance. At these meetings the offenders spoke first; the victims could then tell their own stories and question the offenders. After this the victims could decide for themselves whether to forgive or reconcile themselves with their offenders. Forgiveness, it was understood, could not be requested of the victims by the commission; it had to be freely chosen by the individuals who had been wronged. The processes of applying for amnesty and for receiving forgiveness were related, but they were two different processes.

Pumla Gobodo-Madikizela, a psychologist who sat on the commission, has offered in her memoir, *A Human Being Died That Night,* many examples of the forgiveness process. Let me relay just one that struck me as particularly moving and that illuminates how a person who forgives judges that forgiveness has been merited. The widows of two black policemen who had been assassinated by Eugene de Kock, former head of the South African security police's death squad, by a bomb rigged to their car, came to a meeting at which de Kock was interviewed. After his appearance before the TRC, guarded and in his prison garb, de Kock, known as "Prime Evil" in his assassin days, asked to meet privately with the widows, to whom he offered his apology. As Pumla Gobodo-Madikizela relates: "Both women felt that de Kock had communicated to them something he felt deeply and had acknowledged their pain. [Mrs. Pearl Faku said]: 'I couldn't control my tears. I could hear him but I was overwhelmed by emotion, and I was just nodding as a way of saying yes, I forgive you. I hope that when he sees our tears he knows that they are not only tears for our husbands, but tears for him as well. . . . I would like to hold him by the hand and show him there is a future, and that he can still change.'"[31] Mrs. Faku spontaneously included in her act of forgiveness an invocation of the new beginning, the different future, that a releasing act of forgiveness can make possible—and that repentance prepares the way for. She wanted his change of heart, his repentance, to be the beginning of his reentry into the human fold he had denied and stepped out of. (De Kock was granted amnesty for all his crimes except the two for which he was serving a double life sentence.)

With examples like this in mind, Tutu raised the question in his memoir of whether repentance is or should be a necessary precondition for forgiveness. His answer was that, as in the New Testament parables, unconditional forgiveness, presupposing nothing about repentance, is possible, not just on the grounds of unconditional love; it is also possible for a person to forgive an unrepentant offender because the person doing the forgiving determines that the offender should be restored to the community, or because the offender has died and cannot offer repentance, or because the person doing the forgiving understands that forgiveness offers a release to the forgiver, freeing the victim from the role of being a victim. About this last reason, Tutu comments: "If the victim could forgive only when the culprit confessed, then the victim would be locked into the culprit's whim, locked into victimhood, whatever her own attitude or intention. That would be palpably unjust." But, this said, the most beneficial process of forgiveness for both parties and for their community is one in which the offender repents, as de Kock did: "If the process of forgiveness and healing is to succeed, ultimately acknowledgement by the culprit is indispensable—not completely so, but nearly so." If acknowledgment is not forthcoming, "one day there will be an awful eruption and [the two people] will realize that they tried to obtain reconciliation on the cheap. . . . True reconciliation exposes the awfulness, the abuse, the pain, the degradation, the truth."[32]

People who came to the TRC meetings did sometimes choose not to forgive, but Archbishop Tutu considered this choice only in his pages on the well-known and influential anthology *The Sunflower* edited by Simon Wiesenthal, the Nazi hunter, who had asked contributors to consider what they would do if they found themselves in a situation he had faced: a former Nazi soldier had asked Wiesenthal to forgive him for having gathered a group of Jews into a church and set it afire, burning all his victims to death. Wiesenthal had refused the Nazi soldier's request because he thought that a Jew who had not been caught up in the Holocaust directly had no right to forgive on behalf of those who were killed. Tutu appreciated the argument, understanding Wiesenthal's reluctance to presume to speak for the victims or to seem in any way to diminish the suffering of those who died, or to let a murderer get away with mass murder.

But Tutu himself felt that Wiesenthal's refusal, taken to its logical conclusion, implied that there was nothing the Nazi criminals or the German society could have done after the war or could do now to help the healing process—including making the reparations that Jewish survivors have, in fact, accepted. For Tutu this behavior is contradictory: if they deem themselves able to accept reparations for other people's suffering they should consider themselves able to speak for them as well. Of the South African situation, Tutu argued: "If the present generation could not legitimately speak on behalf of those who are no more, then we could not offer forgiveness for the sins of South Africa's racist past, which predates the advent of apartheid in 1948. . . . True forgiveness deals with the past, all the past, to make the future possible. . . . We have to accept that what we do we do for generations past, present, and yet to come. That is what makes a community a community or a people a people—for better or for worse."[33] I think that Tutu is right, and that communities, just as they have the right and responsibility to bring perpetrators to court, have the right and responsibility to decide whether the perpetrators merit forgiveness. Deceased victims cannot find the truth, tell the story, or make a judgment, so others need to do it for them, in order that community life can go on and not be forever tied to the past. This is what Arendt called mutual release.

The question of who can forgive a mass murderer is moot, of course, for anyone who judges categorically that the Nazi soldier's crime was unforgivable, or that the unrepentant Eichmann's crimes were unforgivable, or that those of any of the unrepentant Nuremburg defendants were unforgivable. What of Arendt's argument that there are *people* who, because of their evil acts, are neither forgivable nor punishable? From Tutu's perspective, it is crucial to the health and healing of a political community—local, state, or international—for its members to hold that *every* person has the possibility to *become* a person who can be forgiven. No one is born evil or, having become a doer of evil deeds, is necessarily fundamentally corrupted and incapable of change, restoration. No one is born banal and thoughtless, or is incapable of being restored to thoughtfulness. No one who becomes dehumanized is incapable of rehumanization or reentry into the human community. The archbishop often made this case in Christian terms, but his appeal is finally to a concept of human plurality that is indigenously African, although it seems to me that the concept he offered in the following passage could well be translated by the word *respect,* which Hannah Arendt had used to translate Aristotle's *philia politike,* or "political friendship":

Ubuntu [in the Nguni group of languages] is very difficult to render into a Western language. It speaks of the very essence of being human. . . . Then you are generous, you are hospitable, you are friendly and caring and compassionate. You share what you have. It is to say, "my humanity is caught up, is inextricably bound up, in yours." We belong in a bundle of life. We say "a person is a person through other persons." It is not "I think therefore I am." It says rather: "I am human because I belong. I participate, I share." A person with *ubuntu* is open and available to others, affirming of others, does not feel threatened that others are able and good, for he or she has a proper self-assurance that comes from knowing that he or she belongs in a greater whole and is diminished when others are humiliated or diminished, when others are tortured or oppressed, or treated as if they are less than who they are. . . . To forgive is not just to be altruistic. It is the best form of self-interest. What dehumanizes you inexorably dehumanizes me. [Forgiveness] gives people resilience, enabling them to survive and emerge still human despite all efforts to dehumanize them.[34]

Considering what has been said and shown about forgiveness for extreme crimes and willed evil by the Truth and Reconciliation Commission, it is very important to distinguish between a court process, which can, as it did in the Eichmann trial, pronounce a perpetrator guilty and punish him (even if any punishment seems dreadfully incommensurate with the crime) and a forgiveness process, including one set in the context of an amnesty process. A forgiveness process would under most circumstances be no substitute for a judicial process, for it cannot fulfill the judicial functions of ensuring that laws are upheld and precedents established, that all are equal before the law, that justice is done. It is also necessary to prosecute people who have had executive responsibility for committing crimes against humanity for the additional reason that, as Arendt pointed out, the nature of such new crimes needs to be established, precedents need to be set that can then become the grounds and guides for legislation. International legislating, which should mean more than the existing United Nations convention on genocide, needs to follow from the existence of international courts, particularly the one now established in The Hague. But judicial processes, despite much popular rhetoric about "closure," do not do what forgiveness can do—release people from the past. They do not have a therapeutic purpose, although they may be therapeutic.

The great lesson of the South African Truth and Reconciliation Commission is that forgiveness and the *ubuntu* or respect that makes it possible need to be cultivated by and in political processes where it is assumed (in Arendt's manner) that forgiveness, as a structural element of human affairs, is a necessity of political life. Adapted to specific local circumstances, forums like the TRC should be as much a part of political life to deal with past conflicts as forums for treaty negotiation—promise making—are to secure against future conflict. Forgiveness is not just an action that can take place, it is an action that must be encouraged; it is not a replacement for judicial process or punishment—that is, not a way of encouraging criminals to act with impunity or a sense that all will be forgiven—but a potential means of preventing endless imprisonment in the past, endless entrapment in horrible crimes. (One of the strongest arguments, it seems to me, against the death penalty is that killing a criminal means that neither the criminal nor the victim can have the benefit of release that comes from forgiveness—and neither can the community. The execution becomes dangerously like vengeance instead of punishment.)

What the lesson from South Africa implies is that in our political structures we should never rule out the possibility of forgiveness for any *person,* no matter how heinous the crime or how great an assault it makes against the condition of plurality, against humanity. When Arendt said of radically evil deeds that all we know about them is that "we can neither punish nor forgive such offenses and that they thus transcend the realm of human affairs and the potentialities of human power, both of which they radically destroy wherever they make their appearance" she, who had the most profound understanding of the nature of human power and its distinction from violence, was, I think, underestimating the potentialities of human power, which includes the power to forgive. A person *always* has the power to forgive, acting in relationship with the one forgiven; such potentiality cannot be radically destroyed unless—through violence—every last person is destroyed.

As Arendt noted, the political significance of forgiveness is harder to recognize than that of promise making because forgiveness has always seemed unrealistic in the public realm, imported from a theological elsewhere, while promise making has always been known to be essential, and to come in many forms: treaties, contracts, covenants, conventions, constitutions. Politics requires laws or constitutions to preserve a space for people to act, but their actual coming and joining together for the time that it takes to act requires the bonding power of mutual promises (or as Jefferson called them in the Declaration of Independence, mutual pledges).

While forgiveness provides *release* from the unpredictability of past human actions, promises provide *respite*—"islands of certainty in an ocean of uncertainty"—from unpredictability as it will inevitably arise in the future. Arendt believed that this respite comes about in two ways: promises allow faith in the face of the basic unreliability of people "who can never guarantee today who they will be tomorrow";[35] and promises allow hopefulness about (if never knowledge of) the outcomes of actions. People who strive for certainty by self-domination or by dominating others are not people who put much stock in promising—or much faith in people or much hope from action.

Arendt's old quarrel with those Romantics who relished the security of a self-made, autonomous self and of an existence independent of confirmation by others, came out clearly as she explained in *The Human Condition:* "Man's inability to rely upon himself, or to have complete faith in himself (which is the same thing) is the price human beings pay for freedom; and the impossibility of remaining unique masters of what they do, or knowing its consequences and relying upon the future, is the price they pay for plurality and reality, for the joy of inhabiting together with others a world whose reality is guaranteed for each by the presence of all."[36] Faith and hope, feelings little admired by the Greeks and Romans, require "the full experience" of the capacity for new beginnings which humans have by virtue of being born, and which the Gospels celebrated with the "glad tidings" of Jesus' birth.

In Arendt's understanding of the modern world, it is in the revolutionary tradition that faith and hope had their translation into political life, where the glad tidings of new beginnings were known—particularly in America—as "public happiness." She points to this phrase as the marker for the unprecedented esteem in which the American founding fathers held not the happiness of private welfare or property ownership but the happiness of being (in Jefferson's words) "a participator in public affairs": "The joys of discourse, of legislation, of transacting business, of persuading and being persuaded" surpassed in the experience of the founders not only any private experiences of well-being or the pursuit of prosperity but any religious experience of God—the traditional Christian contemplative definition of beatitude. Opposition to being ruled by any ruler, enlightened or despotic, was fueled by this passion for public happiness, which a constitution, with its mutual pledges, was meant to preserve beyond the time of the Revolution itself.

Following the lead of the French historian Alexis de Tocqueville, the first historian to compare the French and American Revolutions, Arendt in *On Revolution* tried to identify the basic experiences of the Americans and the French before, during, and after their revolutions, and she found that this public happiness, connected to a "taste for public liberty," was crucial to the American Revolution. Using the method of *The Human Condition,* she described the conditions before the revolutionary action. First, human plurality in colonial America was marked by relative freedom from poverty, even though there were huge discrepancies between the wealthy and the poor; the Revolution did not primarily address matters of social or economic justice. (But she was careful to note that the exception to this condition of relative prosperity was the existence of the slave system, which she often described as the "original crime" of America, the one that the

Constitution did *not* address—preparing through its silence the way to the Civil War.)[37]

The second key condition was that America was not an authoritarian pyramid like France, with an absolute ("divine right") monarch enthroned in the capital and the people below, trapped under feudal organizations. America was a commonwealth full of political associations of many sorts and public meetinghouses in every township—it had a vibrant political life of mutual pledges. Under such conditions, people who were not starving laborers or activists for social justice could focus their sights on winning and instituting freedom from the overseas monarch and rely upon what John Adams called the already existing confidence in one another, and in the common people. The French revolutionaries, concentrating on economic change, violently installed a *party* in place of their king.

In effect, Arendt described two Ideal Types of eighteenth-century revolution, the French and the American, and considered all later revolutions worldwide as successors to only one, the French. She felt that the discoveries and achievements of the American Revolution had not been appreciated in Europe, with its very different economic and social conditions, and that even in America itself there was a tragic "failure of remembrance and thought" that had caused many of its great achievements to be dissipated. Again and again, she pointed to how the revolutionary experiences of the founding fathers had outstripped their ability to liberate themselves from traditional ways of thinking, so that even as they were establishing a secular public realm and realizing that "all authority in the last resort rests on opinion," they were appealing contradictorily to divine authority, a nation "under God." They could announce themselves on the basis of their mutual promises with the resounding, "We hold these truths . . ." and then go on to draw upon the antipolitical treatises of philosophers who did indeed hold truths to be self-evident, absolute, and who could not countenance the idea that the truths that human beings have come to light only in the public exchange of opinions, and their equality is produced only in concerted action. Jefferson may have brought the Declaration to a close with an affirmation of mutual pledges, but he still declared that governments derived "their just powers" from the *consent* of the governed, "and neither he nor anybody else," Arendt commented sadly, "became aware of the simple and elementary difference between 'consent' and mutual promise, or between the two types of social contract theory."[38]

Hardest to recognize, she felt, was how the Americans discovered in the course of their revolutionary action the possibility of securing freedom by a promise—the Constitution—that limited the power that could be generated by any part of the government (Executive, Legislative, or Judicial) or at either level of representative organization (state or federal). The Constitution had even limited the power of the federal government in its relations of promise—its treaties and conventions—with other governments. Marveling at this "greatest innovation in American politics," Arendt noted that the word *sovereignty* nowhere appears in the Constitution. In fact, it explicitly rejects the concept of sovereignty in its Sixth Article, in which the government is held to be an agent of the country; once a treaty is made, it cannot be broken by any citizen within the state, including the leaders, and the country cedes sovereignty under the treaty: "All Treaties made, or which shall be made, under the Authority of the United States, shall be the supreme Law of the Land." (Thus, if the U.S. government signs, say, a Geneva Convention, then the whole of the United States is bound by it—a limitation that is frequently ignored in the present time, when U.S. governments cede not an inch of the sovereignty that they assume they have when they sign treaties.)[39]

Within the republic, the novel use of checks and balances meant that power would not be lost by being submitted to one institution, as it was in revolutions on the French model that ended up replacing an old form of rulership with a new one, a monarchical sovereignty with a party dictatorship. For foreign affairs, it meant that alliances made with other governments would enhance, not detract from, the power of all. Again and again Arendt pressed her point that the founding fathers' discovery rested upon their experience that promises are the means by which acting people can bring about a "truly miraculous enlargement of the very dimension in which power can be effective."

> Power comes into being only if and when men join themselves together for purposes of action, and it will disappear when, for whatever reasons, they disperse and desert one another. Hence, binding and promising, combining and covenanting are the means by which power is kept in existence; where and when men succeed in keeping intact the power which sprang up between them during the course of any particular act or deed, they are already in possession of foundation, of constituting a stable world structure to house, as it were,

their combined power of action. There is an element of the world-building capacity of man in the human faculty of making and keeping promises.[40]

On Revolution is a song of praise to all the state and federal institutions—all the world-building—of the founding fathers that kept the faculty of promising alive and that sponsored the public happiness of expressing opinions and making judgments. At the federal level, she particularly hailed the innovations of the Senate and the Supreme Court. But while she offered praise, she never lost sight of the founding fathers' neglect of the institutions that had grown up in the colonial period before the Revolution and that had made the Revolution possible: the townships and their meeting halls.

Arendt agreed with the great historian of cities Lewis Mumford (in my estimation, one of the few American thinkers of Arendt's generation who was on her level) that the failure to incorporate the townships into either the state or the federal constitutions was "one of the tragic oversights of post-revolutionary political development." This "failure of remembrance and thought" meant that because the citizens did not have local institutions for ongoing, direct participation in the government, they became, for the most part, participators only when they elected their representatives to the state and federal governments. Jefferson did consider in his last years, and in his private letters, how the wards of counties could become "elementary republics," but the importance given to representation through a *party* system as a political principle blocked the emergence of what Arendt thought would have been a truly "new form of government," beyond the republican representational form, which the Americans did achieve.[41]

She called this new form "the council system." And she marveled at the basic similarity between the American pre-revolutionary elementary republics of the townships and the *sociétés révolutionnaires, soviets, Räte,* and councils that emerged spontaneously in Europe, arising out of the revolutionary spirit and actions of people, rather than from theorists. During all the major revolutions, starting with the French and going on through the twentieth-century revolutions in Russia, Germany, and Hungary that she had heard about as a child or read about in her newspaper, councils had appeared that resembled the American ones. Their similarity was, first and foremost, that they had "always been primarily political, with social and economic claims playing a very minor role," even though the overriding concern of the various "French" revolutions was with social and economic claims.[42] But the revolutionary parties pressing those social and economic claims had no theoretical interest in the councils, much less any use for them, and they were eager to stamp the councils out after the fighting was over.

In the last pages of *On Revolution,* Arendt let herself imagine what the new form of council system government might have looked like if it had ever been instituted—or what it might look like in an unknown future. She was obviously not proposing to replace states or federal structures with local councils or rejecting elections and representational government. Her vision was to make all institutions, at all levels of government, be as much like a council as possible and as little like a hierarchy, in which the party in power could dictate policy and appoint administrators. She wanted the voice of citizens to be heard everywhere, not just at election time. In a 1970 essay on civil disobedience in America she wrote that "representative government itself is in crisis today, partly because it has lost, in the course of time, all institutions that permitted the citizen's actual participation, and partly because it is now gravely affected by the disease from which the party system suffers: bureaucratization and the two parties' tendency to represent nobody except the party machines."[43] She went on to suggest that the right of association, which is not granted by the First Amendment, should be written into the Constitution and that—to look at a specific case—civil disobedients could be granted the status enjoyed by registered lobbyists so that they could bring their dissent directly to their representatives.

In *On Revolution,* she envisioned a cadre of experienced political actors winning trust in the emergent local councils and then rising via "self-selection in the grassroots political organs" to the next level of council and then to federal councils. She described this vision with the Ideal Type metaphor she had developed for distinguishing a totalitarian onion from an authoritarian pyramid: "No doubt this form of government, if fully developed, would have again assumed the shape of a pyramid, which is, of course, the shape of an essentially authoritarian government. But while, in all authoritarian government we know of, authority is filtered down from above, in this case authority would have been generated neither at the top nor at the bottom but *on each of the pyramid's layers* [emphasis added]; and this obviously could constitute the solution to one of the most serious problems of all modern politics, which is not how to reconcile freedom and equality, but how to reconcile equality and authority."[44]

In the decades since Arendt's death, her appreciation of the power of promising and the potestas in populo of the council system have seldom been taken seriously by contemporary political theorists, most of whom cannot imagine a political life that is not organized primarily around electing representatives to governments which then dominate their citizens. Her appreciation of the council system is said to be the unrealistic or utopian streak in her thinking. But Arendt's vision has been embodied in an action, now visible retrospectively as a whole, the story of which would make as fitting an epilogue to *On Revolution* as her epilogue on the Hungarian Revolution made to the 1958 edition of *The Origins of Totalitarianism*. In its very name, Solidarity, this action—this creating of councils—testifies to the power of promising.

The memoir by the 1984 Nobel Peace Prize winner, Desmond Tutu, tells the story of the Truth and Reconciliation Commission as a new beginning. What the repercussions from this action will eventually yield is a matter for future actions to show, but the discovery, made in action, that truth can come into the light of the public domain through a process of forgiveness is now a world-building event. Solidarity's action was recognized by the world when the 1983 Nobel Peace Prize was awarded to its leader, Lech Walesa, but that recognition was part of the unfolding action, for Walesa used his forum in Stockholm not just to present Solidarity to the world, emphasizing its commitment to nonviolence, but to make an appeal to the Communist government of Poland—and behind that, the Soviet Union—for a political space for speech and action. While comrades from Solidarity sat in prison, Walesa used his international forum to call for an end to the martial law that had been imposed on the Poles, breaking a remarkable mutual promise.

Solidarity's nonviolent strike at the Lenin Shipyard in Gdansk had resulted in that promise: the 1981 General Agreement in which the government had permitted free trade unions the right to strike and granted limited freedom of religious and political expression. This promise had redressed more than a decade of frustration, which began early in 1968, when the government had stifled the student movement at Warsaw University, sending many students and one of the key leaders, Jacek Kuron, to jail. At the same time, an international student movement was gathering momentum throughout Europe and the United States. But in August, Kuron, still imprisoned, was forced to reevaluate his thinking, as were the students across Europe, when the armies of the Soviet Union and its Warsaw Pact allies crushed the councils that had sprung up among students and dissidents within the Czechoslovak Communist Party. (Arendt, in Switzerland visiting a seriously ill Karl Jaspers, could hardly bear to read the news of the collapse of the "Prague Spring." She wrote to her husband, telegraphically: "The newspapers—Czechoslovakia. It's all horrible.")[45]

The memory of August 1968 became key to Kuron and his fellow students in Poland as they reassessed their situation. They had learned the lesson that relying on reformers within the Polish Communist Party (PCP) would be futile. But most important they had learned that violence against a Communist government—and thus, by extension, the Soviet Union—was clearly impossible; it would just increase the repression. The response to the violence would be more violence—tear gas, tanks—that would buttress the repressive regime still further. One of Kuron's protégés, Adam Michnik, explained this lesson in his *Letters from Prison,* in which he rejected the model of the French Revolution that was, so Arendt had argued, the only model known in Europe: "By using force to storm the existing Bastilles we shall unwittingly build new ones." (This was the practical political judgment that expressed Arendt's thought: "The practice of violence, like all action, changes the world, but the most probable change is to a more violent world.")[46] With the Polish students' rejection of violence a new chapter in the history of revolutions opened.

The opposition Polish intellectuals turned their attention in the mid-1970s to resisting the PCP's authoritarian control over every facet of life by sponsoring "self-rule" (the term was borrowed from Gandhi's program for developing habits of initiative and discipline at the local level in India) and "self-organization" outside the party. The idea was to build a real, day-to-day community of free people —what Arendt would have called a council system and likened to the township organizations of pre-revolutionary America. People practiced in politics would then be able to put pressure on the government from below. Alliance was sought with the Catholic Church, which, even though it espoused an old-fashioned nationalism, had supported civil liberties for all Poles; and alliance—solidarity—was sought with the workers who had, before they were repressed in 1970, won some concessions from the government by a series of strikes. A Charter of Worker's Rights was drawn up in 1976 by a Workers' Defense Committee made up of dissident intellectuals.

By August 1980, when Walesa, an electrician by trade, and his co-workers in the Lenin Shipyard went out on strike, Poland was alive with community organizations, and people from many walks of life were prepared to support Solidarity. The membership reached ten million by 1981, at the time of the General Agreement, but then the Polish president General Wojciech Jarulzelski, on orders from the Kremlin, imposed martial law and Solidarity was formally dissolved by the Parliament. A lean seven-year period of regrouping, organizing, and thinking followed, and it was during that period that Michnik in Warsaw and his associates at the journals *Krytyka* and *Res Publica* established, in conjunction with intellectuals in Budapest associated with the journal *Beszelo,* the Democracy Seminars, which were forums for discussions of how a transition to democracy could take place. American scholars at the New School for Social Research sponsored the Democracy Seminars and shared their discussions, sending to Warsaw and Budapest copies of the first book the groups wanted to discuss in their clandestine meetings: Hannah Arendt's *Origins of Totalitarianism.*[47]

On the basis of their understanding of the nature of totalitarian regimes, Michnik and his comrades devised a strategy to insert a democratic election process into the existing political structure, which was slowly undergoing a process of detotalitarianization, and over the years this strategy was reinforced by the actions of the workers' councils, which reemerged to mount further strikes and urge government recognition of Solidarity. This was finally achieved, and eventually Solidarity even put up candidates for free elections to the bicameral Polish Parliament, which was headed by a president from the Communist Party and an elected premier.

Solidarity's election victory was overwhelming, and in 1989 Tadeusz Mazowiecki, a journalist and Solidarity strategist, became the first non-Communist premier to govern Poland since the late 1940s. But he and Walesa differed over the question of how and at what pace Poland should convert to a market economy, and by the time Walesa was elected president of Poland in 1990 the union's solidarity was beginning to unravel, particularly because Walesa's views became more and more those of a traditional, pre-war Polish nationalist, an advocate of parties, not councils. Many political parties emerged in Poland during the early 1990s, and the phenomenon Arendt had observed in all the French-type revolutions appeared again: the party system overwhelmed the council system. But because the revolution had been nonviolent, the party system that triumphed was not a system of vengeance and violence, and it was not a one-party dictatorship but a multi-party system. A great deal of genuine and lasting reform had been instituted.

By that time Solidarity's example had spread not just across Eastern Europe, where it eventually helped spur the nonviolent "velvet revolutions" of 1989, but into the Soviet Union. In 1985 Mikhail Gorbachev, at age fifty-four, had taken over the Soviet helm from a string of aged, deteriorating leftovers from the Stalinist era: Brezhnev, Andropov, Chernenko. These leaders had presided over the deterioration of the Soviet economy and the kind of breakdown of technological infrastructure that produced the world's first major explosion of a nuclear reactor at Chernobyl in 1986. After initially lying about the reality of the Chernobyl disaster, Gorbachev made an unprecedented, televised speech in which he told an astonished population the truth about the accident. It was as though Gorbachev were demonstrating the lesson of the great manifesto of the velvet revolutions, the essay "The Power of the Powerless," by the Czech writer and dissident Václav Havel, which argued that those who are able to "live in the truth" and emerge from a life "within the lie" would open up "singular, explosive, incalculable political power."[48]

Gorbachev had made the momentous decision to hand the Soviet people the truth, to let them face the reality of the hundreds of dead and sickened in Chernobyl, only the first toll of a vast environmental crisis. Gorbachev acknowledged that the Soviet people had been left out of the rising tide of prosperity and high technology that was changing America and Europe, including Eastern Europe. And with his message came two Russian words that were quickly spoken all around the world and recognized as the contemporary heritage of Solidarity and its revolution: *glasnost* and *perestroika*.

Gorbachev's policy of glasnost produced such a swift exit from life within the lie that the Soviet school history exams for 1988 had to be cancelled: the students' history books were obsolete because so many lies about the past had been exposed, so many heroic leaders from Stalin onward had been relabeled murderous totalitarians. The new openness and repudiation of lying was far more thoroughgoing than Khrushchev's thaw, and it was communicated to the people not just by a suddenly flourishing publishing community but also on television and in the cinema. As the Soviet government's archives were opened to scholars, the Poles received in 1989 compensation for their long suffering at the hands of the Soviets in the form of the truth about the 1939 mass murder of Polish soldiers at Katyn, which was proven to be—and acknowledged by the Soviet government to be—the responsibility of the Soviets.

Gorbachev recognized with his perestroika policy that the Soviet people should become more responsible for their economy and their government, but he never appreciated the Polish emphasis on self-rule or the council system; he thought that the Communist Party should stimulate and guide the reorganization of society he envisaged. Although it was not dictatorial, his "revolution" was also not derived from the people, so it had the complicated effect of encouraging truth-telling and free speech without sponsoring the kinds of forums in which people unpracticed at being what Jefferson called "participators in public affairs" could help one another face their pasts and make mutual pledges. Rather, Gorbachev's reforms had a polarizing effect, setting Western-oriented progressives against Stalinism-oriented reactionaries; nationalist and ethnic backlashes became ferocious, particularly as the regime made an imperialist drive into Afghanistan; and the heritage of pain and suffering that had accumulated over fifty years of Stalinism and post-Stalinism poured forth in streams of blame.

Gorbachev himself could not follow his own liberalizing vision, for it had never included placing real confidence in the people but had always been based on his confidence in himself and in the party reformers he had gathered around him. But these were not people who had risen from local political organizations or been schooled in a council system, and they were out of touch with the mood of the country. When Gorbachev finally lurched toward alliance with the antireform Stalinist conservatives in the party, opponents of the Russian leader Boris Yeltsin, he found that these conservative stalwarts had no use for him. Instead, they declared a state of emergency and deposed him as president. But this attempted coup had a short life—three days. The antireformers had no opportunity to engage in violence because the army and even the KGB, so important in its heyday to Stalin's totalitarian dictatorship, went over to the forces lined up behind Yeltsin. And the Soviet Union disappeared—the most dramatic moment in the long history of detotalitarianization.

Solidarity's inspiration also reached to other countries of Eastern Europe: early in 1989 the Czechs and the Hungarians were able, using the original Polish council system model, to organize and rise up nonviolently against their own Communist governments, which were no longer backed by the Soviets. Hundreds of thousands of East Germans left their stifling country, which West German governments tended to refer to as "the lost eastern territories," crossing over the opened borders into Czechoslovakia and Hungary. Meanwhile, many of those who remained joined protests in the streets of Berlin, under the shadow of the wall that had divided the city since 1961. In November 1989, East Germans were able to cross into West Germany through holes made in the Berlin Wall by the protesters and their sympathizers on the western side. After its fall and the events that came to be called collectively "the Central European Revolutions of 1989," a truly unprecedented moment was at hand for the emergence of Europe as a political entity.

When Arendt had written in the "Concluding Remarks" of the first (1951) edition of *The Origins of Totalitarianism* about her hope for a comity of nations, she was aware that the French foreign minister Robert Schuman, inspired by the visionary Jean Monnet, had already proposed integrating the coal and steel industries of Western Europe; the year her book was published the European Coal and Steel Community (ECSC) was set up with six members: Belgium, West Germany, Luxembourg, France, Italy, and the Netherlands. Monnet became the first president of a supranational body called the High Authority that could make decisions about the coal and steel industries in these six countries. The member states moved to dissolve trade barriers among themselves after 1957, when the Treaties of Rome had created the European Atomic Energy Community (EURATOM) and the European Economic Community (EEC). By 1967, the existing European institutions had merged and a European Parliament had been set up as the political institution for the EEC. The parliament's representatives were chosen by the national parliaments of the members until 1979, when an unprecedented election took place: citizens of the member states directly elected representatives to the European Parliament.

The events of 1989 propelled forward the increasingly political European efforts, which had grown out of the successes of the economic initiatives; and those events also created states that could apply for membership in the growing EEC, which had begun accepting new Western European members in 1973. The EEC was not a council system of the sort existing in America before the Revolution, but it did rely on a series of international working groups, commissions charged with making reports, specific recommendations, and general proposals for treaties. These discussion groups, which usually bore the names of their chairs, were made up of political representatives from the member states as well as of civilian experts—economists, bankers, lawyers, security professionals, environmentalists, agricultural specialists, and so forth—in all the areas to be affected and regulated by the growing union. The commissions were not spontaneous meetings of citizens, not elementary republics, but they were and still are forums for exchanges of opinion, for preparing the way for promises.

The Treaty of Maastricht, signed in 1992, established many new forms of cooperation between the member governments—chiefly in the areas of defense and "justice and home affairs"—and launched the more politically named European Union. With this treaty Europe, which for almost two centuries had been the home of revolutions that followed the French model, underwent a completely nonviolent "American" revolution.

This astonishing demonstration of the power of promising fueled a further momentum of promising that has progressively taken down trade, travel, currency, and education barriers between the member nations, very much attuned to the realities of the world we live in. The policies adopted commonly by the E.U. members have adjusted, for example, to the growing awareness in Europe of environmental issues—an awareness that was so sadly lacking in the Soviet Union as it dissolved and that has been slow to emerge in the independent republics that succeeded it. For example, the original aim of the E.U. agricultural policy was to produce as much food as cheaply as possible, but then, as the general standard of living improved, it evolved into providing support for farming methods that produce healthy, high-quality food while protecting the environment. This shift eventually spurred concern for environmental protection across the whole range of E.U. policies. Environmental protection is, in Arendtian terms, a clear sign that the human condition she called "earth"—the condition that humans live upon the earth together and share it as their common home—has been recognized *politically.*

In retrospect, it is clear that the 1968 upheaval in Europe and then the emergence by 1980 of Solidarity exposed the weakness (the powerlessness, in Arendt's terms) of Poland and the other Warsaw Pact states and their master, the Soviet Union. The revolutions that followed in 1989 were conditioned by those weaknesses as well as by the courageous actions of people who took creative advantage of them. When the council system that Arendt had so admired in its earlier incarnations before the Second World War and in Hungary in 1956 reappeared in various forms, it accounted for the most important revolutionary achievements. The velvet revolutions, which mixed features of the American and French revolutionary models Arendt had delineated, evolved into a new type of revolution, unknown to her, that proceeded nonviolently before focusing on constitutional reform. Meanwhile the four-decades-long revolution that resulted in the European Union, which these national developments fed, produced a novelty: an American-style revolution resulting in a federation of nation-states—nation-states that have agreed to relinquish the elements of national sovereignty that stood in the way of their union.

But the Europeans had not emphasized politics at the beginning of their revolution. The clear distinction between economic and social concerns and political concerns that Arendt had considered definitive in an American-type revolution was not, for the Europeans, as strict as Arendt had made it out to be. And in the world we live in now, more than three decades after her death, the socioeconomic and political domains *cannot* be distinguished as strictly as Arendt had distinguished them, for they are, in daily life, too intertwined. Her distinction should function now as a constant reminder of how crucial it is for the political domain to be, as much as is possible, the domain for decision making about economic and social concerns, and how crucial it is for political discussion and decision making to be different from what goes on in corporate boardrooms and free, as much as possible, from corporate influence. The Europeans were able to address the poverty and economic inequality of individuals, classes, regions, and nations with organizations for economic cooperation, and then, on the basis of that achievement (and a much-contested, intricate arrangement for continuing to aid states with standards of living below the E.U. average), move toward political union. And now—only now—the Europeans face the great challenge of writing and ratifying a constitution, state by state, on which all European citizens will vote. The ratification process is currently deeply contested, particularly because there is no totalitarian Soviet Union looming to the east to galvanize the Europeans into a defensive solidarity. Indeed, more Europeans fear the superpower looming to the west, across the Atlantic Ocean, not because it is totalitarian but because it is not interested in mutual promises and because, in its unilateralist assertion of sovereignty, it is coming to resemble Hobbes's Leviathan. (In Latin America, which might be the next region to follow the model of energy and economic integration laying the groundwork for political union, shared opposition to U.S. economic and political dictation has led a new generation of national leaders to envision a Latin American Union.)

The transformations of the Soviet Union and Europe, West and East, have been miraculous, but they have not, of course, erased the past or obliterated the legacy of totalitarianism. The post-Soviet states and the new Europe are constantly being threatened by old, prewar nationalist aspirations (in which state sovereignty is the goal), ethnic struggles, and the growing diversity of their populations. Even in states where the council system was originally strongest and most influential, the revolutionary spirit of people participating in public affairs is not as well protected by constitutions and treaties as it needs to be. Perestroika in the Soviet Union had the least possibility of survival because it was a top-down system and did little to encourage public happiness. That legacy conditions politics in the former Soviet Union states, where revolutionary struggle, as in Ukraine, continues and violence is all too common, particularly repressive violence emanating from Russia. Everywhere, nationally and internationally, the old challenge that Arendt had identified so clearly—how to keep the citizen participators in public affairs participating and exerting upward the pressure of their nonviolent exchanging of opinions and mutual promising—remains. And everywhere the forces longing for old forms of top-down authority and old visions of violence "making history" weigh against the power of the people. The legacy of totalitarianism is the specter that haunts the former Soviet Union states and the states of the new Europe.

Even Arendt, certainly the greatest appreciator in the postwar period of the power of the people and their new beginnings, had not been optimistic about Europe before 1968. And I think it can be instructive to step back, knowing what has resulted from the events of 1968 and their tremendous aftermath, and examine the causes of her worry. She did not live long enough to see even the beginning of the new political Europe or the end of the old Soviet Union, but she did, in the last years of her life, see the crucial antipolitical specter that threatens the political institutions that have evolved in the lands that once succumbed to Nazism and Stalinism. And she did live long enough to identify the same trend in America. Her constant concern in the last decade of her life was the crises of the republic.

I shall begin this exploration of Arendt's concern by focusing on a little-known text of hers from 1967. I have concentrated thus far on the sections of *The Human Condition* that deal with action, the power of forgiving, and the power of promising. But *The Human Condition* is also a book that, long before the word *globalization* appeared to mark a new reality, was concerned with human society as a whole in the post-totalitarian period; and it is in this globalizing societal-technological context that the crises of the republic she examined are taking place.

Before 1968, Karl Jaspers, who was well known throughout Europe for his prescient *Atom Bomb and the Future of Mankind* (1958), had been one of the few Europeans to sound the alarm about the way the legacy of totalitarianism was deforming Europe, especially West Germany. In 1966 he had published *Wohin treibt die Bundesrepublik?* [Where Is West Germany Headed?] and after it became a best-seller had followed up with *Antwort* [Answer], aimed at his critics in the West German establishment who were trying to pacify the public he was seeking to rouse. After arranging to have the two books translated and edited into a single volume, *The Future of Germany,* for American readers, Arendt wrote a foreword for the new book in which she summarized his judgment and stressed how dangerous it was for Americans, preoccupied with the war in Vietnam, to ignore the drama unfolding in the Bundesrepublik.

Arendt knew that the main thesis of this "politically most important book to appear in Germany after the Second World War" would shock American readers, and she hoped that the shock would be strong enough to stimulate them to agree with Jaspers and the two other German public intellectuals—Rudolf Augstein, publisher of *Der Spiegel,* and the novelist Günter Grass—who could see clearly what was going on. Their shared opinion was that "the Federal Republic of West Germany is well on the way to abolishing parliamentary democracy and may be drifting toward some kind of dictatorship."[49]

A former high-ranking official in the Nazi Foreign Office, Kurt Kiesinger, had just become chancellor of West Germany; and in the same election the National Democratic Party (NDP), an extremist right-wing group, had surged into prominence, bringing with it people who proclaimed that international Jewry, not Hitler, had been responsible for the outbreak of the Second World War. The German finance minister Franz Josef Straus saluted the NDP for its redemptive patriotic nationalism. (The NDP was a forerunner of the anti-Semitic and more generally anti-immigrant right-wing parties that are influential now, particularly in France and Austria.) Meanwhile, the two major West German parties, the Christian Democrats and the Social Democrats, had made a grand coalition that would allow them to silence opposition. Arendt, with her usual eye for novelties, identified the coalition as a "new form of government": not the one-party dictatorship of protototalitarian states, but "a kind of two-party dictatorship," or, in Jaspers's phrase, a "dictatorship of politicians."[50] Eventually an "emergency law" was adopted by this new form of government, which, if it had been effected, would have annulled the constitution. Like all such emergency laws (including the USA Patriot Act of 2001, passed by a nearly unanimous two-party vote) the emergency law handed the government over to its Executive branch and eroded many civil liberties; but its distinction, and greater threat, came from the fact that there was no emergency at hand, as there was in the United States in 2001.

As Arendt stressed, Jaspers did not indulge in simple analogical thinking and argue that "Bonn is Weimar," nor did he think that another Nazi movement would arise; but he did reject the defensive cliché emanating from the government that "Bonn is *not* Weimar." His judgment was that there were elements in the government that were "conspicuously similar to those that characterized the last months of the Weimar Republic" before Hitler won the chancellorship. Trying to make clear the novelty of the new situation, Jaspers wrote that "the very threat which in the Weimar Republic came from anti-state forces in search of revolutionary change lies now in the state itself. . . . The [state] transforms itself, vaguely pursuing the very aims that were pursued in those days: authority, authoritarian state, dictatorship."[51]

As Grass had warned repeatedly, this drift in German politics was profoundly alienating to left-leaning young Germans. He had feared that, as they found themselves living in a dictatorship of politicians, they would embrace left-wing extremism, a counterpole to the right-wing extremism of the nationalists in the NDP. And this did happen in the short run as the disaffected young people—to the astonishment of most of their elders—became leaders in the European student rebellion. But even though they preached violent revolution and spoke in extremist Marxist-Leninist clichés, the students also turned out to be solidly opposed to the Weimar-like features of the government in Bonn. Their movement opened a space for others who shared Jaspers's opinions to come forward. Far more powerfully than a single book could have, they got a public discussion going—through concerted action, in public meetings and demonstrations—about Germany's past and its future. And because the students would not tolerate the lie that had sustained Germany in the postwar years, namely, that (in Arendt's summary) "the Germans were never really Nazis," they moved forward the incomplete process of "mastering the past," a process that would certainly have benefited from a Truth and Reconciliation Commission had such a thing been known. Although it was not innovative as a political institution, the student rebellion saved Germany from its drift toward dictatorship. During the revolutionary period of 1989, when the Berlin Wall came down, that movement was finally halted. Helped by the emergence of the Green Party, a genuine political party of the left, leaders from the generation of 1968 could rise up through the local and state governments to federal office and, after 1992, into political roles in the European Union.

One of those former student leaders was Daniel Cohn-Bendit, known in Paris as Danny the Red before he was expelled from France in 1968 and continued his activism in Germany. During the time of the German dictatorship of politicians, Cohn-Bendit, who was the son of friends of Arendt's and Blücher's from their Paris exile in the 1930s, studied *The Origins of Totalitarianism* because, as he said later in an interview: "[In the early 1970s] I was perplexed by the reluctance [among Germans] to compare communism with national socialism, which was rooted in German history."[52] For Cohn-Bendit, as an anti-Communist leftist, it was crucial not to lie about what the two totalitarianisms had had in common and not to expect that communism would solve Germany's problem. By 1984 Cohn-Bendit had found his base in the Green Party and eventually he became co-chair of the Greens in the European Parliament, a post he still holds.

Cohn-Bendit's evolving focus reflected something that Arendt had observed (uniquely, I think) about the worldwide student movements in the late 1960s. Her 1969 analysis in *On Violence* is worth quoting at length because it shows, again, her emphasis on novelty:

The new militants have been denounced as anarchists, nihilists, red fascists, Nazis, and, with considerably more justification, "Luddite machine smashers," and the students have countered with the equally meaningless slogans of "police state" or "latent fascism of late capitalism," and, with considerably more justification "consumer society." Their behavior has been blamed on all kinds of social and psychological factors—on too much permissiveness in their up-bringing in America and on an explosive reaction to too much authority in Germany and Japan, on the lack of freedom in Eastern Europe and too much freedom in the West, on the disastrous lack of jobs for sociology students in France and the superabundance of careers in nearly all fields in the United States—all of which appear locally plausible enough but are clearly contradicted by the fact that the student rebellion is a global phenomenon. A social common denominator of the movement seems out of the question, but it is true that psychologically this generation seems everywhere characterized by sheer courage, an astounding will to action, and by a no less astounding confidence in the possibility of change. But these qualities are not causes, and if one asks what has brought about this wholly unexpected development in universities all over the world, it seems absurd to ignore the most obvious and perhaps the most potent factor, *for which, moreover, no precedent and no analogy exist* [emphasis added]—the simple fact that technological progress is leading in so many instances straight into disaster; that the sciences, taught and learned by this generation, seem not merely unable to undo the disastrous consequences of their own technology but have reached a stage in their development where "there is no damn thing you can do that can't be turned into a war . . . " In short, the seemingly irresistible proliferation of techniques and machines, far from threatening certain classes with unemployment, menaces the existence of whole nations and conceivably of all mankind.

. . . In [Nobel laureate] George Wald's words, "what we are up against is a generation that is by no means sure that it has a future." For the future, as [Stephen] Spender [in *The Year of the Young Rebels*, 1969] put it, "is like a time bomb buried, but ticking away, in the present." To the often heard question[,] Who are they, this new generation? One is tempted to answer, Those who hear the ticking. And to the other question, Who are they who utterly deny them? The answer may well be, Those who do not know, or refuse to face, things as they really are.[53]

In this analysis, which complements what Jaspers had written in *The Atom Bomb and the Future of Mankind*, Arendt was sounding the second deep chord of warning in *The Human Condition*. This warning joined her warnings about philosophical and governmental hostility to the people's action. Let us recall her lecture remark of 1954: "The world's central problems today are the political organization of mass societies and the political integration of technical power."[54]

Action can be obscured by a philosophical prejudice against it and all but eliminated by state domination of the people, in tyrannical, authoritarian, or totalitarian governments. But action can also be threatened when labor and work become so dominant in the vita activa that action has no place, its relative absence hardly noticed by those who think about politics only in terms suitable for labor and work, and who glorify the relentless progress of the consumer-technological society.

Arendt had argued in *The Human Condition* that in the post-totalitarian world a "consumer society" or a "technological society" or a "laboring society"—she used the three terms in different contexts—was emerging that was unique in history. The word *society* for her referred to a modern, post–Industrial Revolution realm, neither public nor private, in which labor and work were evolving into activities for supplying not the necessities of life but an unprecedented superfluity of goods and techniques for making more goods, including destructive goods. This society, she went on to argue, was also evolving in a paradoxical manner: because of technological progress, particularly in automation, many laborers were being liberated from the grueling, mind-numbing forms of labor typical of the Industrial Revolution, but they were not thereby being liberated from the mindset of laboring. Nor were they being freed for the possibility of engaging in higher forms of thinking and judging, which would require that they be educated anew, lifted out of the mass society of those who had no opportunity to distinguish themselves, reveal who they are. On the contrary, most people in a consumer society think of themselves as laborers, mere jobholders, even artisans and those engaging in acting or thinking activities. They are all "making a living," doing what they think of as supplying necessities (even when those "necessities" are not in any way necessary for life). People who are "making a living" cannot, in Arendt's terms, distinguish themselves in freedom or really think about what they are doing; they are only doing a job. A bureaucracy is a good place to become a thoughtless person, but any job will do as long as the person doing it is only doing a job.[55]

Arendt pointed to another dimension of this situation that is also crucial: many of the scientific creators of advanced technological goods are also doing their jobs, and they also do not consider it part of their job to think about what they are doing. They operate, Arendt explained, with "truths" that can be demonstrated in mathematical formulas and proved technologically (that is, translated into technologies) but cannot be spoken of "conceptually or coherently" in the kind of words that make up political discourse or the exchange of opinions—that is, the kind of words in which people would discuss what the scientists are able to do and make. She drew the political implication sharply: "If it should turn out to be true that knowledge (in the modern sense of know-how) and thought have parted company for good, then we would indeed become the helpless slaves, not so much of our machines as of our know-how, thoughtless creatures at the mercy of every gadget which is technically possible, no matter how murderous."[56]

Know-how in the 1950s, when Arendt was writing *The Human Condition,* had produced the nuclear bombs that the students of the 1960s heard ticking, but also other forms of what looked to Arendt like unprecedented challenges to the human condition as it had been experienced until that time. Human beings were experimenting with putting objects in space—*Sputnik* was launched in 1957—and imagining space travel; that is, they were longing to leave the earth and the condition of being creatures who live upon and share the earth. They were imagining creating life in a test tube and making genetically improved human beings by artificial insemination. This longing to control natality was matched by a desire to control mortality by extending the normal life span (not just curing diseases). She catalogued all these challenges, but always returned to focus most intensely on nuclear weapons because they, of course, pose a threat to the whole of the human condition—to life, to earth, to worldliness, to natality, to mortality, to plurality.

Arendt did not explore the motives for these forms of "rebellion" against the human condition (although that is the very political word she used), but she did make it clear, in the 1950s and for the rest of her life, that the modern split between thinking and both the "making a living" mentality of laborers and the know-how orientation of scientific workers was the context in which the fate of action had to be considered. Specifically, she thought that the kinds of deteriorations that can take place in nontotalitarian states or post-totalitarian states—which were all deteriorations in the direction of dictatorships of politicians—involved, crucially, what she called "image making," that is, the importation into political life of the commodity production techniques (and marketing) of consumer society and the know-how thoughtlessness of modern science and technology. The politicians of deteriorating republics are, she thought, people who are doing their jobs and treating political decision making as if it were scientific calculation or application of theory.

A dictatorship of politicians was exactly what Arendt saw America drifting toward in the early 1970s, and she took it upon herself to do as Jaspers had done: sound an alarm. She did so in a speech, "Home to Roost," that was delivered at the Boston Hall Forum to mark the upcoming bicentennial of the American

Revolution.[57] Arendt argued in this colloquially titled speech that two key totalitarian elements had appeared in the "years of aberration" during the Vietnam War and through the "ignominious defeat" America had suffered (which she insisted upon honestly calling a defeat). The first was the need to maintain an image that bore no relation to reality, and the second was the need to lie in the service of that image. Invoking the long piece she had written in 1971 on the Pentagon Papers ("Lying in Politics"), Arendt stressed that the political leaders who had launched the U.S. military escalation in Vietnam and defended it with lies right up to the end were defending an image of invincible American military might. Their image was of "the mightiest nation on the earth" and nothing—no lost troops, no wasted resources, no civilian casualties—was more important than that image and what came to be called "credibility," which meant the capacity to live up to that image.

A totalitarian ideology, she had long argued, required terror for its reinforcement and its extension into every aspect of the private and public lives of friends and foes, but maintaining an image required something more banal: public relations, the "hidden persuasion" techniques of Madison Avenue, and carefully orchestrated lying. Both terror and image selling have in common that they entail lying on principle and that they involve the intrusion of criminality into politics. But image selling is the mild totalitarianism of dictatorial politicians, who undermine the state from within by selling an image of security and protection (a Leviathan image) for which the citizens pay with their power, and by founding that image on a lie (which will connect to many derivative lies).

Although image selling may not be "the cruelest" form that the deterioration of political life can take, and people tend to judge it as not too serious because they are analogizing it to the cruelties of totalitarian total terror, image selling can corrupt the whole of political life. It is truly a banality of evil. In her 1975 speech Arendt noted: "The ultimate aim of this terribly destructive war, which [President] Johnson let loose in 1965, was neither power nor profit, not even anything so real as influence in Asia to serve particular tangible interests for the sake of which prestige, an appropriate image, was needed and purposefully used. This was not an imperialist politics with its urge to expand and annex. The terrible truth to be gleaned from the story told in [the Pentagon Papers] was that the only permanent goal had become the image itself. . . . Image-making as a global policy is indeed something new in the huge arsenal of human follies recorded in history."[58] This sounds frighteningly familiar to us now because that image, of "the mightiest nation on earth," reinforced by the disappearance of the rival Soviet superpower, again guides our global policy, and it is subscribed to by two political parties that have lost what once distinguished them from each other, and also lost their interest in debate with the Executive. But the image as it is being deployed now also has a new emphasis, deeply resented around the world: the mightiest nation on earth, and most able to teach—or impose—God-given democracy.

Following her standard procedure of isolating the novel aspect of a phenomenon, Arendt stressed that the U.S. government bureaucrats had received from their own intelligence services all the information they needed to make an accurate assessment of the situation in Vietnam before the war and during the steady escalation of that war, and they ignored it. She observed that the "non-relation between facts and decision, between the intelligence community and the civilian and military services, is perhaps the most momentous, and certainly the best guarded, secret that *The Pentagon Papers* revealed." Summarily, her judgment was: "One sometimes has the impression that a computer rather than 'decision makers' had been let loose in southeast Asia. The problem solvers did not judge; they calculated."[59]

Arendt often said that it was Eichmann's thoughtlessness that propelled her in her last years to write the "Thinking" section of *The Life of the Mind.* But she was spurred to write the "Willing" and "Judging" sections of her great book by her deep, long-meditated insight that the intellectual crux of antipolitics—the intellectual origin of totalitarian dictatorships and of dictatorships of politicians in republics—is lack of respect for, and absence of, judgment. When willingness to impose an image has replaced imagination, when calculation has replaced judgment, the life has gone out of politics.

three

Thinking About
*The Life of the
Mind*

Each of Arendt's books and essays contains a reflection on how *not* to think about the topic she is going to consider. She had introduced *The Origins of Totalitarianism,* her field manual for comprehending a novel form of government, with these somber sentences, which reject prophetic thinking: "This book has been written against a background of both reckless optimism and reckless despair. It holds that Progress and Doom are two sides of the same medal; that both are articles of superstition, not of faith." A few pages later, she commented again on how not to think: "Comprehension [later she would say *judgment*] does not mean denying the outrageous, deducing the unprecedented from precedents, or explaining phenomena by such analogies and generalities that the impact of reality and the shock of experience are no longer felt. It means, rather, examining and bearing consciously the burden which our century has placed upon us—neither denying its existence nor submitting meekly to its weight. Comprehension, in short, means the unpremeditated, attentive facing up to, and resisting of, reality—whatever it may be." In the late 1950s and 1960s, when she was less despairing herself and more able to draw upon the cautious optimism of her amor mundi to write *The Human Condition* and *On Revolution,* Arendt rejected the conceptual legacy of political philosophy and offered instead a "new science of politics" with a primer of new concepts adequate to "think what we are doing."[1]

In the last years of her life Arendt turned her attention to the human mental activities in a much more sustained and systematic way. In *The Life of the Mind,* she looked back on the entire

Western philosophical legacy of investigation into how we think, will, and judge and rejected almost all of it. Conducting a conversation in her own mind with the few exemplary philosophers who, in her opinion, had been able to face reality, to be at once philosophers and political people, citizens, she wrote not a new science of politics but a new vision of how philosophy and politics could be reunited. She moved from her project of thinking what we are doing to the project of asking what we are doing when we think, when we will, and when we judge.

While she was writing *The Origins of Totalitarianism,* Arendt had thought that the most pernicious perversion of thinking and judging was ideological reasoning, which invoked the future of Nature or History and worshiped Progress, as though the future—the Thousand Year Reich—were something that could be seen or known. But in the early 1970s, when she was more alarmed than she had been since the end of the Second World War, she became convinced that people do not have to subscribe to future-oriented ideological supersense or jump the constraints of ordinary logical thinking to lose touch with the realities of the world. Something much more banal would do, which she came to call "an image," which we can define here as a projection onto the future of a present unreality, a piece of potentially violent wishful or willful thinking.

Arendt's experience during the controversy in the 1960s over her *Eichmann in Jerusalem* had given this insight a personal dimension. She realized that those who conducted a campaign against her and her book first created an image of her book—an image that actively denied the reality of what she had written—and then marketed that image, diverting discussion to the image and away from what she had written. Later, as she faced up to Germany's descent into "two-party dictatorship" and America's conduct in the Vietnam War, she refined her sense of how image making is done and has its effects, particularly how it depends upon and perpetuates a fundamental lie, a denial of reality. "The Germans were not Nazis." "The North Vietnamese attacked us first." Today we could add, "Iraq has weapons of mass destruction."

Identifying a novelty, in this case a particular kind of lying and lack of judgment, always led Arendt to a philosophical question. "What are we doing when we judge?" was the question that went along with the "What is thinking?" question that Eichmann's thoughtlessness had raised for her. At the same time that she was writing her sharp critiques of image making in American politics as a lack of judgment similar to thoughtlessness, she undertook what is certainly her most challengingly difficult book, *The Life of the Mind,* and it is to that book that I want to turn now, viewing it as her warning. We can read it as a very political work of philosophy.

The Life of the Mind, which Arendt once called "a kind of second volume of *The Human Condition,*" is the most difficult of her books to read and think about for a number of reasons. For one, she did not live to finish it, and the almost fully drafted "Thinking" and "Willing" parts of the manuscript, even though they were beautifully edited after her death by her friend Mary McCarthy, do not have the systematic clarity she could have brought to them had she been able to revise them. The third, never-written part, was to have focused on judging, and it was really the book's raison d'être: the earlier parts on thinking and willing were to serve its purpose, much as what she had said in *The Human Condition* about laboring and working served the purpose of recovering action from conceptual neglect. In *On Revolution,* while describing how, over the course of their deliberations, the American founding fathers had come to envision the Senate as a "lasting institution for opinion" and the Supreme Court as a "lasting institution for judgment," she had noted that opinion and judgment are the two "politically most important mental faculties," but they have been "almost entirely neglected by the tradition of political as well as philosophical thought."[2]

When she made this observation, Arendt had already begun a study of the great exception to the rule of neglect of judgment, Kant's *Critique of Judgment,* the last of his trilogy of critiques, published in 1790, soon after the French Revolution. Karl Jaspers's luminous study of Kant, which he had just added to the gallery of his *Great Philosophers,* confirmed her, she had told him in 1957, in her feeling that in the third critique, "Kant's real political philosophy is hidden."[3] So a reader of *The Life of the Mind* has to imagine both her unwritten "Judging" section and what she had found hidden in her Kantian source. I shall try to take us on such a voyage of the imagination in the pages following.

But before we set off, let me note that there is another quality in this last book of hers that makes reading it an experience of something not quite brought into the open, something hidden, private. The book intensely reflects her conversations with the philosophical men—living and dead—who mattered most to her, and there are emotional chords in it of both joyfulness and mournfulness associated with these relationships. She was conversing with Heidegger in "Thinking" and "Willing," where she delivered her rejection of his unworldly equation of the two; in the "Judging" lecture notes, Kant, Jaspers, and Heinrich Blücher were her sounding boards. I know this, too, from my own memories of that period.

In the fall of 1970, more than a year after Jaspers's death at the age of eighty-six in Basel, Arendt offered two courses at the New School for Social Research: a lecture on Kant's political philosophy and a seminar on *The Critique of Judgment*. Jerome Kohn and I took those courses together, and we could see, at the beginning of the semester, that she was conducting a kind of conversation with Jaspers. (Later, when she suggested that I write a doctoral dissertation surveying Jaspers's philosophy, she told me that she often imagined conversations with him "over all these Kant things.") In my estimation, the book of Jaspers's she most engaged with then was his *Origin and Goal of History*, first published in 1949, just as she was finishing *The Origins of Totalitarianism*.

The very title of *The Origin and Goal of History* situated Jaspers the thinker between past and future; it is the book in which Arendt's teacher most clearly engaged with Kant's vision of history "with a cosmopolitan intent." Jaspers had explored concretely, empirically, the period between 600 BCE and the Hellenistic empires that preceded the Roman Empire, when, among the peoples of China, India, Persia, Palestine, and Greece, sages, prophets, and philosophers had appeared who thought *freely*, standing outside their inherited mythic traditions and imagining the possibilities of human action, new beginnings, and new relationships among peoples of a shared world, a *cosmopolis*. Jaspers had then asked how the contemporary descendents of these visionaries—we, the book's readers—might call upon their "Axial Age" example. One way would be to question critically how the modern Europeans, Americans, and Soviets, with their scientific achievements, their know-how, and their technological innovations, had come to dominate the world, producing both the conditions for a new period of global unity and communication and the conditions that had led to totalitarianism and the Cold War. How could a new world order—not a world government, which would inevitably be a plurality-denying world tyranny—come about on the basis of a common understanding of the possibilities and the perils of the "one-world" technological reality, defined by the existence of both global communications and the global threat of nuclear devastation? In 1949, just as the long march to the European Union was beginning in the rubble of the devastated European nation-states, Jaspers had imagined federations of states that had renounced complete sovereignty, and in 1951 Arendt had responded to him by invoking her comity of nations.

Arendt's conversation with Jaspers colored her Kant courses at the beginning of that fall semester in 1970, but in the middle of the semester the courses changed. Arendt's husband, Heinrich Blücher, died suddenly of a heart attack, and she was gone for the weeks of his funeral and memorial services, the beginning of a mourning that did not really end until her own death five years later. When she returned to class, shaken, trying to control her smoking, looking very frail in her black *Witwentracht,* it was obvious that her thoughts were never far from Blücher. The materials she left for the "Judging" part of *The Life of the Mind,* which grew out of those Kant courses, had, I think, the hidden purpose of being her *laudatio* (a eulogy whose task it is to praise the man) for Blücher, as well as her lamentation.

Like Jaspers, her husband had been for her a model man of good judgment, an example. As she argued beautifully in her notes, judgment does not follow rules but always needs examples, presented to it in imagination. Further, Blücher's good judgment had behind it a passion for Socratic thinking, which she had already discussed at length in an essay called "Thinking and Moral Considerations." In this essay, which became the first segment of *The Life of the Mind,* she alluded to lectures about Socrates that Blücher himself had given at Bard College, one of which is published now in *Within Four Walls,* their correspondence. Arendt's last book began as their collaboration and it went forward after his death as their collaboration in her mind. To encounter *The Life of the Mind,* and to ask why it matters for us in our technologically unified world, we have to imagine this conversational life of her mind.

On the basis of her experience, Arendt said that judgment, more than any of the other mental abilities, is exercised in relationships with others. It involves visiting others—physically or in your mind—and consulting them, seeing things from their point of view, exchanging opinions with them, persuading them, wooing their consent (in Kant's lovely phrase). A judgment appears in the world as an opinion, where it joins, as it also reflects, the plurality of opinions that are in the world. Having this kind of communicative experience, this "enlarged mentality" (as Kant called it), mentally or in the world or both, allows a person to transcend the subjectivity and privacy of perceptions and come to what is known as common sense. (Kant's term was *sensus communis,* the common human understanding of something, as opposed to *sensus privatus.*) Just as acting together gives people the "enlargement of power" that none can have alone, *Urteilskraft* (which means, literally, "judgment-power" not just "judgment-craft" or the art of judgment) gives them an experience of the world and of other people that makes them mentally powerful; well-traveled; not isolated but connected; not provincial but cosmopolitan. Judgment is the faculty that prepares a person to be the Kantian ideal: a world citizen.

One might say in other terms that judgment, more than any of the other mental abilities, fits us for the condition of human plurality and is rooted in it (as action is "ontologically rooted" in natality). As Arendt stressed, judging presupposes being able to see what the world is like from another's perspective. This does not mean adopting another's judgment or agreeing with another's opinion, or even empathizing with another's experience or reading his or her mind. It simply means using your imagination to see things from another's standpoint. (Judging and imagining are linked abilities, as we shall see later.) In a lecture called "Some Questions of Moral Philosophy," which Jerome Kohn edited, Arendt had noted: "The more people's positions I can make present in my thought and hence take into account in my judgments, the more representative [my judgment] will be. The validity of such judgments would be neither objective and universal nor subjective, depending on personal whim, but intersubjective and representative. This kind of representative thought, which is possible only through imagination, demands certain sacrifices; Kant says, 'we must so to speak renounce ourselves for the sake of others. . . .' [We] are considerate in the original sense of the word, we consider the existence of others and we must try to win their agreement." Kant was the first philosopher to praise cosmopolitanism and imagine what world citizenship might entail because he had such an appreciation of the sensus communis. As he wrote, sounding Arendt's later critical theme of Romantic self-absorption: "Egoism can be opposed only by plurality, which is a frame of mind in which the self, instead of being enwrapped in itself as if it were the whole world, regards itself as a citizen of the world."[4]

Judgment comes in many different varieties, operating in many different spheres—cognitive, scientific, aesthetic, moral. But generally speaking, it always involves finding a relation between some form of particular and some form of generality. For example, I just noted that there are particular forms of judgment but that something can be said about them generally: they all fit under the rubric "judgment relates particular and general." In Kant's terms, I was proceeding *reflectively:* I was saying there are various particular types of judgment but if you look carefully into all of them, you will find that they have something in common.

But we can also judge *deductively,* starting with a generality and going to a particular. In the cognitive domain, for example, when we perceive something particular, say, a bridge, we have in our minds a general schema (that is Kant's word) of a bridge that enables us to say, "This is a bridge; this is a particular instance of that general schema." A similar operation takes place in the moral domain whenever we have accepted an existing rule (usually a negative one like "Thou shalt not kill") from which we want to deduce a particular course of action (I can't kill this person). Logical reasoning, using syllogisms, also operates deductively. You might use syllogistic reasoning to say "all roses are beautiful; this flower is a rose; hence it is beautiful."[5] But, of course, if you exclaim, "This is a beautiful rose!" you do not—unless you have spent far too much of your life in a Philosophy Department—operate in this syllogistic way, because "This is a beautiful rose!" is an aesthetic judgment and, as Kant's *Critique of Judgment* shows in detail, aesthetic judging operates reflectively, not deductively. Aesthetic judging is not a matter of general schemata or application of rules.

Aesthetic judging begins when a particular phenomenon strikes you. It becomes what the French call a *chose vue* and, having caught your attention, it sets you wondering and simultaneously makes you aware of yourself as someone who is trying to arrive at a judgment. What shall I make of what I have seen (or touched or heard or smelled or tasted)? Kant noted that the sensation of taste has traditionally supplied the metaphors for judgment generally: we taste something, we subjectively enjoy or do not enjoy the taste (which is like tasting ourselves), and then we approve or do not approve our taste. (This last step of reflectively judging our judgments can operate in all kinds of judging.) To communicate our judgments, we say, "This tastes good," or "This is the best-tasting dish," or, metaphorically, "Ah, to my taste this is the best painting or the best play!" Taste (like smell and somewhat like touch, but unlike sight and hearing) is inherently discriminating; it is so at one with its objects that it enjoys or does not enjoy them on contact, as it were. So, more than sight or hearing, which have more distance from objects, taste must make an effort to rise above the immediate subjective it-pleases or it-displeases discrimination if it is to arrive at judgment and then at approval or disapproval of judgment. The effort to achieve distance or room to judge is undertaken by imagination, which deals in *representations* of sense objects. Imagination sets objects up in our inner world to be thought about, but it also makes the objects ready to be internally "sensed" and reflected upon approvingly or disapprovingly: the reflective judging activity. (Imagination is like a virtuoso servant, assisting thinking, willing, and judging to step back from or recoil from the world: it also sets images or objects before the will for choosing or deciding upon.)

The recoil from the world in aesthetic judging constitutes its freedom, but also gives it a kind of impartiality, what Kant called "disinterestedness," by which he meant an affirmation of the existence of something that does not entail wanting or needing to use it or to control it or dominate it. Impartiality, disinterestedness, and communicability each present a crucial feature of reflective judgment. Impartiality is particularly important for historians and storytellers, as it allows them to recognize, for example, the experience of both sides in a war, to sing of the Achaeans and the Trojans, the Greeks and the Persians, the Christians and the Muslims (an impartiality that is certainly needed now, even more than in ancient times).

In making his distinction between deductive and reflective judging, Kant showed himself an astute diagnostician. A person who cannot make deductive judgments is stupid, he said. Any intelligent person should be able to fit a particular to an existing generality, to say, "This is a bridge," when looking at a bridge, or "This is a rose," when selecting a flower—or, to take a more complex illustration, "This is a dictatorship," when looking at a regime in which a person or a party commands the obedience of all, controls the military and the media, and suppresses dissent. What happens to stupid people is that they become caught up in an infinite regress, not knowing what rule to follow in applying just this schema or just this generality to a given particular; not being able to depend upon rules for applying rules. In his diagnostician mode, Kant remarked dryly (and with uncharacteristic pessimism) in a footnote that I cited earlier: "For stupidity there is no cure."[6]

On the other hand, a person is not stupid, but rather *insane*, claimed Kant, who cannot make reflective judgments. Experiencing a particular sensation and then stepping back from it, representing it and reflecting on it, comparing it to what is known about it in the sensus communis, enjoying the "enlarged mentality" of judging, approving and disapproving; these are essential qualities of sanity. Persons who lack them are persons in "a frame of mind in which the self [is] enwrapped in itself as if it were the whole world."[7] Contemporary psychiatrists seldom acknowledge it, but Kant's diagnosis anticipated their understanding of insanity, based on the work of Freud: a psychotic person is one who cannot recognize reality, cannot become oriented in space and time, and is not mentally connected to other people; the mind of a psychotic is enwrapped in itself as if it were the whole world. For insanity, fortunately, there are cures, therapeutic and political, both sorts of which involve overcoming world-alienation, reconnecting to people and to a shared world. There is nothing like the enlargement of power experienced in shared action or lively discussion to bring people back to the common world.

If a person who cannot judge reflectively is insane this means, of course, that the ability to judge reflectively is a key characteristic of sanity. And Arendt carried this thought out to a remarkable extreme: in effect, she argued that the ability to make the enlarged mentality of judgment a feature of life by forming a circle of friends made up of contemporaries and people from the historical or literary past is the mark of a person's ability to live well. The circle of friends should themselves be good or powerful reflective judges; they should be exemplary judges—and the person choosing them should be able to judge them as such. Judgment is the loom of friendship.

Arendt, Jaspers, and Blücher—a small circle of friends—were all drawn to the *Critique of Judgment* not because they were especially concerned with aesthetics but because they were convinced that what Kant had discovered about aesthetic judging, and about reflective judging generally, was directly transferable into the domains they were concerned with: political judging and moral judging. Kant himself held the opposite view about moral judging. He believed that moral judging was and should be deductive: there is, ultimately, a general rule, a categorical imperative that should be universal (accepted by all, applying to the species as a whole), that could be applied whenever anyone wanted to know what to do in a particular instance. People should act so that a maxim of their actions could become a rule for all humankind.

Arendt was always impressed that when Kant was considering the greatest event of his day, the French Revolution, as a moralist, an applier of moral rules, he had opposed it. No one who followed his categorical imperative, the centerpiece of his *Critique of Practical Reason,* would engage in revolutionary action, for this would involve saying that one was willing to make revolutionary action (and violence) a rule for humankind. But when he was observing the Revolution as a spectator, he was tremendously enthusiastic about it, finding it thrilling that the whole world was watching its events, an enlarged mentality was being created. Considering the sympathy that he and so many spectators felt, Kant even wondered whether their sympathy reflected a moral predisposition in the human race for freedom. As a spectator, he realized, along with other spectators, the importance—the novelty, the unprecedentedness, the revolutionariness—of the Revolution.

When Arendt considered Kant's divided reaction, she asked herself whether understanding his feelings as a spectator—his excitement and pleasure in action—would enable her to understand political and moral judging. She was assuming that these kinds of judging did not generally follow rules or proceed deductively. A political judgment like "This is a two-party dictatorship" might come about deductively if the schema or concept or sum of the elements of all kinds of party dictatorships were known, but often—particularly in relation to unprecedented phenomena— political judging must proceed reflectively, looking for the generality, the concept, as she was doing in her analysis of Germany's novel two-party dictatorship in the late 1960s. Similarly, if the commandment "Thou shalt not kill" were accepted, or if the categorical imperative were subscribed to, a moral judgment like "Do not kill this person" might be arrived at deductively. Moral rules would apply as they do in the realm of repetitive behavior, which is not action, where all is new and unpredictable. But deduction would not be possible if the rule were not accepted or if the rule for applying the rule were not known. Arendt realized, of course, that many people do want to accept moral rules or even a single imperative, but she thought that under the historical conditions in which all moral rules that have ever been promulgated have been rendered useless or worse by events, it makes no sense, and can even be dangerous, to try to decide what to do on the basis of moral rules and deductions.

What good is a moral rule, a commandment, like "Thou shalt not kill" when it is obvious that a regime can grow up in a Christian country where this rule is supposed to apply but where, instead, killing becomes the order of the day, the de facto rule, and total terror reigns? Did this rule or any other, Arendt asked herself, guide those in Germany who were able to resist the totalitarian regime and refuse to do its killing work? What did enable the resisters to resist? What enabled Jaspers to resist? If Jaspers and the other resisters were not following rules, how were they making their judgments? She also put her question the other way around: as she listened to Eichmann at his trial recite Kant's categorical imperative while perverting Kant's intention by substituting his Führer's will for the rule that should determine the actions of all humankind, she asked herself whether this man ended up doing evil because he was such a devoted and submissive conformist to the rules du jour.

We shall return to the domain of moral judgments, but I want to underscore here that when Arendt explored the manner of judging that Kant called reflective, she was also exploring her own manner of political thinking and judging. Reflective judgment can begin from a particular that needs to be combined with other particulars to reach a generality, but it may also begin from a particular that does not turn out, upon examination, to fit into a generality. For example, in Montesquieu's *The Spirit of the Laws,* Arendt found a catalogue of forms of government: democracy, oligarchy, monarchy, tyranny—government by the many, by the few, by the one, by the tyrannical one—each animated by a particular principle, each predominated by a particular virtue, each containing a key fault or shortcoming. (Montesquieu, in effect, created schemata for recognizing governments.) But when she studied totalitarianism, she discovered that it did not fit under any of the general types in Montesquieu's manual and, further, it did not fit the commonly accepted generality that all governments involve rule by one person or one group over another. This was an unprecedented "government by nobody," a particular form of government that destroyed all political life, an antipolitical politics. In effect, *The Origins of Totalitarianism* supplied a schema (the Ideal Type) for totalitarianism. Similarly, she studied revolutions and created two schemata—American-style revolutions and French-style revolutions—which can allow us, in our own historical period, to recognize Solidarity and the Central European velvet revolutions of 1989 as particulars not subsumable under these schemata, as unprecedented.

Arendt's greatest gift as a political thinker was to identify novelties, to explore them, and when the exploration led to a generality, to state that generality clearly. She could reflectively judge particulars of a high level of complexity, taking more elements of the particulars into account than most of us can even remember, much less distinguish. Late in her life, she exercised her gift over the faculty of judgment itself by pointing to the image-making American officials in the Vietnam era whom she described not just as thoughtless but as not-judging, judgmentless. They did not judge; they calculated; they proceeded deductively from their false premises. She was looking at and reflecting on the refusal to judge reflectively, the desire to rely on generalities or theories (like the domino theory), and the willingness to fabricate particulars where there were none, that is, to lie.

Most of the notes and lectures that Arendt made for the "Judging" part of *The Life of the Mind* are rethinkings of Kant's insights into aesthetic judging (and, more generally, reflective judging), and transfers of those insights, thus rethought, into the domains of political and moral judging. But while she was doing this, she was also continuing her old struggle against the prejudices of philosophers—prejudices to which even Kant succumbed in trying to imagine the political and moral domains as rule-bound.

We can see what her complicated work yielded if we revisit the notes and lectures with a guiding question: What do people who are able to judge reflectively, to be judging spectators, contribute to the political domain?

In the *Critique of Judgment*, Kant had considered the makers of aesthetic objects, artists. In Arendt's terms, artists are fabricators, with a capacity for originality. Artists need spectators to clip the wings of their genius and make it communicable to people who are not geniuses (that is, the rest of us). Actors, with their capacity for novelty, for new beginnings, also need spectators to make their actions communicable by talking about them, analyzing them, and ultimately telling stories about them (upon which some day an artist will draw to tell the story that renders the actions a meaningful event). What fabricators make and actors do would never appear, become communicable, and be communicated if there were no judges or spectators making judgments: "The judgment of the spectators creates the space without which no such objects could appear at all. *The public realm is constituted by the critics and the spectators* [emphasis added] and not by the actors or the makers. [Although] this critic and spectator sits in every actor and fabricator . . . spectators exist only in the plural. The spectator is not involved in the act, but he is always involved with his fellow spectators. He does not share the faculty of genius, originality, or the faculty of novelty with the actor; but the faculty they have in common is the faculty of judgment."[8]

Arendt recognized that Kant had discovered the mental condition for the constitution of a public realm, the condition supporting the political condition, which is that laws open and preserve the public space where actors can act, generating power, and fabricators can memorialize those actions. In mental terms, powerfulness in the public realm is measurable by the number and quality (in terms of communicability and interactivity) of the critics and spectators that keep it going. If people spoke without judgment, in total unison, about the actions, for example, of their government, this would be a sign of political insanity; and when politicians call for such unison, trying to preclude discussion and dissent, they are—from this point of view—dictators.

Because the enlarged mentality and the sensus communis make up powerful judging, a judgment which arises from one mind alone (a self enwrapped in itself as if it were the whole world) is not powerful, in the sense that it will not be representative or persuasive to other people (although it may be inflicted upon them). Others will not feel that their positions are taken into account by a narrowly based opinion; they will not be able to connect with it, and they will not be inclined to move toward it, to agree with it upon reflection if they do not agree at first. Persuasiveness is the mark of judgment-power, Urteilskraft. But one might also say (as neither Kant nor Arendt did explicitly) that a single-minded, isolated judge makes potentially violent judgments, ignoring, excluding, or erasing other people's viewpoints; arrogant and presumptuous judgments; or, to speak psychodynamically, narcissistic judgments. Plato, so hostile to anything but reasoning, the most abstract form of thinking, characteristically saw things the other way around. For him, Arendt noted, "persuading the multitude means forcing upon its multiple opinions one's own opinion; thus persuasion is not the opposite of rule by violence, but is only another form of it."[9]

A person with Platonic prejudices would never come to the conclusion that an ability to question one's own view and judgment, to keep one's opinions under review in light of new experiences and new encounters with the judgments and opinions of others, is a desirable ability. But this self-questioning (so different from self-doubt) is another key characteristic of powerful judgment. The exercise of this ability is, however, quite rare, for a reason that was well known among the non-Platonic Greeks and Romans, who gained experience interacting with people through their empires. Their insight was wryly summarized and applauded by the sixteenth-century French essayist Michel de Montaigne in his "Of Presumption": "It is commonly said [among the ancients] that the fairest division of her favors Nature has given us is that of sense [*sens*]; for there is no one who is not content with the share of it she has allotted him."[10] Because we all think that we are able to sense clearly, it takes a special effort for someone to "see beyond his sight" (in Montaigne's phrase). And that effort is judgment.

The less an experience is communicable, the more it is assumed to be indisputable. So aesthetic judgments, which are often assumed to be matters of taste and nothing more (that is, they are assumed to be completely subjective), are frequently said to be indisputable (indeed so frequently said that "de gustibus non est disputandum" is one of the few Latin maxims that does not need translating). But neither Kant nor Arendt emphasized the incommunicability or difficulty of representing taste, although they acknowledged it. Rather, they stressed what moves us to make the special effort of representing our experience and of overcoming the privacy of taste (attaining common sense), and that is that we do not enjoy tasting alone. Tasting is inherently sociable, intersubjective, something to talk about. Only the world-alienated like to eat alone; most people find it hard to enjoy a meal without company, any more than they like to go to the theater alone, without someone with whom to discuss the play. On the other hand, people have no trouble retreating from company to think or to meditate. Arendt's "spectators exist only in the plural" is really a way of saying that judging is a form of public happiness.

Despite the Latin maxim, which really refers to a common form of insanity, not a condition to applaud, people do, in fact, dispute about judgments of taste, taking great pleasure in so doing, and they certainly dispute about political judgments as a feature of their public happiness. But it is true that their disputes do not end in truth. And this, from Arendt's non-Platonic point of view, is as it should be. She was not disappointed that opinions, expressions of judgment, are not final truth and that dispute or discussion does not end in truth. She felt that their open-endedness was part of their nature inasmuch as they have their roots in human plurality.

As it is in the nature of action to be unpredictable and without end until the actors have left the stage and the storytellers (exercising their judgment) have turned the action into an event, it is in the nature of judging to be unpredictable and without end at all. Everyone knows that even a judgment that has been laid down or instituted can be taken up or reinstituted later, as a story told can be retold, which is one reason why Christians await a Last Judgment, hoping that there will be from God a final accounting more definitive than the one humans can make, even after death, when the story of a life can be told.

The unpredictability of judging and the unending nature of judgments or opinions have proven just as hard to tolerate in most of the Western tradition as have the unpredictability and unending nature of action. The Roman Pliny's maxim (of which Montaigne was fond) that "there is no certainty but uncertainty" feels to many like a cynical sign over an abyss. Just as Plato's hostility to the active life had a profound effect upon how the active life has been regarded ever since, his hostility to opinion (*doxa*) has made it almost axiomatic that opinion is a pale imitation of the truth, which appears only to a solitary truth-seeker's contemplative gaze. As his famous allegory in the *Republic* has it, opinions exist in a dark cave of deceptive appearances where the benighted multitude sit enchained, while truth is higher, outside the cave in a realm of light, where only those freed from worldly chains can go. The public realm, where citizens and professional opinion-mongers (sophists) trade their wares (sophistries), is a realm without truth.

Most philosophers, sharing this opinion (and it is an *opinion*) of opinions, have not explored or even inquired about—or even named—the human capacity to form opinions, that is, judgment; they have only tried to avoid exercising the opinion-forming capacity, to stick with reason, which supposedly leads to truth, and to pour scorn on any form of relativism. When this attitude prevails, not only is the domain of judgment and exchange of opinions obscured, but crucial distinctions between types of truth are lost.

First to be obscured are factual truths. These may always have a touch of subjectivism about them, a bit of perspective built into them, but as Arendt, who so often wrote about the importance of facing reality, facing facts, used to say to those struggling to define a fact: "Look here, it is a fact that in 1914 Germany invaded Belgium; it is not true that Belgium invaded Germany." Less easily obscured are logical or mathematical truths of the $2 + 2 = 4$ variety that are verifiable in themselves and require no reflective judgment. Cognitive or scientific propositions have a different status: they are provisional, lasting until they are proven false or their provisional status becomes apparent when a paradigm shift in the scientific field reveals them to be more wrapped in prejudice or pre*judgment* than their discoverers realized.

But another matter altogether are those truths claimed to be absolutely true, absolutely not-opinion, by moralists or philosophers; and it is in debates (that is, exchanges of opinions) over the status of this kind of truth or this kind of truth-claim that the philosophical strategy is deployed of denigrating those (like Arendt) for whom such truths are really matters of judgment and (relatively true) opinion. Such denigration is the philosophical version of a strategy we are accustomed to in the political sphere: accusing a person who questions how things are run in the *patria* of philosophy, the land of truth, of being unpatriotic.

Among the Greeks of Plato's time, many nouns were available for different kinds of reasoning or thinking, but no noun existed for the capacity to form opinions, although Greek has a large number of verbs derived from the verb *dokein,* to give an opinion, that deal with different kinds of judging (assaying, estimating, examining, scrutinizing, judging character, testing for fitness, reaching verdicts in a courtroom). But the Greeks did have a word, not related to the word *doxa* (the noun derived from *dokein*), that covers part of what Arendt meant by judgment: *phronesis,* which Aristotle specifically said is the insight of the political person into affairs of the polis. "Such insight," Arendt explained, "into a political issue means nothing other than the greatest possible overview of all the possible standpoints and viewpoints from which an issue can be seen and judged."[11] Arendt thought that Aristotle's exploration of judging was limited by his assumption that phronesis deals with goals of action imagined as given and knowable (that is, his lack of appreciation for reflective judgment), but she did credit him with being the lone precursor of Kant's enlarged mentality, which Kant himself did not recognize as a political ability.

For a positive evaluation of political judging, the Western philosophical tradition did have to await Kant, who knew not what he offered, although in the less lofty and formal precincts of essay writing (which literally means writing judgments, writing *essais*), no one was more respectful of judgment than Montaigne, who explored his own judgment (called sometimes *jugement,* sometimes *entendement*) more thoroughly than any writer before him, reveling in the pleasure of such an examination: "I continually observe myself, I take stock of myself, I taste myself. Others always go elsewhere, if they stop to think about it; they always go forward (No man tries to descend into himself—Persius); but as for me, I roll about in myself."[12] This Montaigne, such an enthusiast for self-examination, and such an admirer of the world's greatest self-examiner, Socrates, held that the human soul (*esprit*) has many facets and features and faculties, but that only a soul in which judgment takes the lead can be said to be in harmony with itself and happy. (Note that he did not say "reason" or "faith.") For happy people of good judgment, Montaigne had a beautiful designation that recognizes that a good judge refuses self-deception: *honnêtes hommes*.

It is certainly no accident that Montaigne was also the great exemplar in his time of cosmopolitanism and openness to what we would now call multicultural diversity. In his remarkable essay "Of Cannibals," for example, he reports on what he has learned about the native societies of the Americas from several indigenous American visitors to France. He details impartially the admirable naturalness of their ways, commenting on how the natives' way of life was impossible for most Europeans to appreciate because "each man calls barbarism what is not his own practice." Montaigne was, uncharacteristically for his day, aware that the natives (like later colonized peoples) had learned from their European conquerors many of the practices that most Europeans condemned; adopting, for example, the Portuguese practice of flaying their prisoners of war alive rather than eating them after they had killed them. "I am not sorry that we notice the barbarous horror of such acts, but I am heartily sorry that, judging their faults rightly, we should be so blind to our own. I think there is more barbarity in flaying a man alive than in eating him dead." Writing during the worst days of Catholic and Protestant wars in France, Montaigne noted that he had himself witnessed "among neighbors and fellow citizens, and what is worse, on the pretext of piety and religion" acts of cruelty and torture that made the cannibalistic wartime practices of the Indians seem more civilized.[13] This was Montaigne realizing that the clearest mark of poor judgment is provincialism, not being able to see beyond your own practice, which always leads to hypocrisy or holding another to your standards when you do not respect them yourself.

Montaigne also knew something further about judgment that Arendt conceptualized clearly: judgment needs, first and foremost, examples, exemplary figures. In the Renaissance manner, he sought examples in Greco-Roman antiquity, and she, too, noted that when people of the European tradition judge, for example, courage, they think of Achilles or Hector. But she also noted that different cultures and political traditions look to different examples for standards or criteria, which are abstractions or schemata drawn reflectively from particular examples. In *The Spirit of the Law,* Montesquieu had shown that the different forms of government he catalogued had different animating principles: "Montesquieu was probably right in assuming that each such [political] entity moved and acted according to a different inspiring principle, recognized as the ultimate standard for judging the community's deeds and misdeeds—virtue in republics, honor and glory in monarchies, moderation in aristocracies, fear and suspicion in tyrannies—except that this enumeration, guided by the oldest distinction between forms of government (as the rule of one, of a few, of the best, or of all) is of course pitifully inadequate to the rich diversity of human beings living together on the earth."[14] Good and powerful judges will self-consciously appeal to such an ultimate standard, but they will also both realize—as a product of their enlarged mentality—that different communities have different standards and be respectful of the differences, aware that each standard reflects a shared experience and history.

In the Western political tradition, there is not much conceptualization of judgment, but since Montaigne, and certainly since the Enlightenment, there has been less prejudice against judgment and opinion in the political tradition than in the philosophical tradition, where there is so much lamenting that they are not reason and truth. As Arendt had pointed out in *On Revolution,* revolutionary actors have been particularly free of the philosophical prejudice because of what their actions have taught them: "Historically speaking, opinion—its relevance for the political realm in general and its role in government in particular—was discovered in the very event and course of revolution. This, of course, is not surprising. *That all authority in the last analysis rests on opinion* [emphasis added] is never more forcefully demonstrated than when, suddenly and unexpectedly, a universal refusal to obey initiates what then turns into a revolution. To be sure, this moment—perhaps the most dramatic moment in history—opens the doors wide to demagogues of all sorts and colors, but to what else does even revolutionary demagogy testify if not to the necessity of all regimes, old and new, 'to rest on opinion'?"[15]

I have been making preliminary sketches of judgment, based on various discussions of it in Arendt's books, letters, diary entries, lecture notes (and my own friendly respect for Montaigne). But to judge why her analysis of judging matters, we need to look at the other two mental abilities she explored in *The Life of the Mind*, thinking and willing.

She never offered any justification for saying that humans have these three main abilities and, presumably, no others, any more than she had offered an explanation of why labor, work, and action make up the vita activa. Certainly, she was guided by the way Kant had parsed the mind into pure reason, practical reason, and judgment in his three critiques, but as I have indicated she did not follow him in what she had to say about any of his three abilities (not even about judgment, where she owed him the greatest debt). More fundamentally, as any reader of her book, even in its unfinished state, would become aware, she thought of each mental ability (she sometimes used the English word *faculty*, which meant to her the German word *Vermögen*, "power," "capability," "ability") as crucial to experiencing one of the three dimensions of time. Thinking relates us to the things of the world in the present, as we encounter them, and via imagination produces representations or "after-thoughts" of them for the other mental faculties to work with. Willing is our "organ" for the future. And judging connects us to all the judgments or opinions of people as they have been made and as they exist within our traditions, our archives, the memory precincts where we find examples of human worth. Judgment both calls upon precedents in the same way judges do in a court and identifies what is without precedent and needs a new law or explanation, as judges do in case law.

By pointing to the temporal orientations of the three faculties, I am suggesting that they should be considered in the context of their interrelations: the life of the mind is the life not of one faculty, but of all. Their interrelations provide checks and balances (to draw explicitly the political analogy that Arendt often used implicitly). A political unit with free checks and balances has wise legislators for thinking and considering opinions, an executive for willing, and a judiciary for judging actions and forming opinions. But the unit is most powerful when each branch is made up of people who have capacities for all three activities and councils where the exercise of all three activities is encouraged. Similarly, a mentally free individual allows the three free faculties a rich interaction.

Each faculty manifests the characteristic that all, in Arendt's view, have in common: they are all autonomous, which means that they are all free. The faculties do not derive from or owe obedience to a single source that acts like a sovereign over them, and none of the three follows any rules except those inherent in its own activity. Chiefly, they are all self-motivating, free from domination or determination by the world or by phenomena in the world, because all operate by spontaneously recoiling from the world. They become divided internally and then are healed of their internal division.

Thinking, she argued, is not tied to appearances in the world as are sensation or perception and intellectual cognition—these are "intentional," absorbed with and by an intended object. You look at human beings in order to know them; you scientifically analyze, explore, and classify them, working toward general understandings; but you *think* about what it is to be human and what the meaning of human life is. You devise "thought-things," concepts, for conducting this thinking. Perception and cognition come to results (knowledge); thinking searches for meanings. Thinking's quest, Arendt held, is endless. It does not come to rest except in those who give it up, interested only in results. Contemplatives also experience thinking as a coming to rest, but for them it does not rest in a result; it rests in a vision or an intuition or a passive beholding of an object not of this world.

For Arendt, as for Blücher, Socrates was the model thinker, and his experience of thinking (which you can find in Plato's dialogues if you read past the Platonizing and pay attention to what Socrates himself said and did) provided the definition or schema Arendt applied: "Thinking is the soundless dialogue [*dialegisthai* as 'talking through words'] between me and myself."[16] This soundless dialogue has the immediate effect of liberating us from not only conventional "truths" but conventional rules of conduct because the thinker wants above all to keep the thinking dialogue going. That is the "goal" of thinking: to keep thinking. The dialogue will not keep going if it comes to rest in a truth or if it becomes a scene of hostility, the result of one member of the "me and myself" partnership doing something the other does not want to live with. From the point of view of the "thinking ego," as Arendt called this site of dialogue, it is better to suffer wrong than to do it and have to live with the wrongdoer.

Thoughtlessness, then, is the absence of internal dialogue. A person (like Eichmann) who "does not know that silent intercourse" hears no objections or has somehow ceased to hear objections about a possible wrongdoing, and thus can live with the wrongdoer. When people hear no objections to doing evil within themselves, and, further, hear no objections from outside, under conditions in which "everybody is swept away unthinkingly by what everybody else says and believes in," they are prepared to do what everyone else is doing—including commit murder, or even mass murder. These banal people are very different from (and potentially much more dangerous and destructive than) a rarer type, wicked people (radically evil people, in Kant's terms), who, rather than not hearing their thinking partner, hear it but overcome it, silencing all objections.[17] These people are tyrants in themselves, to themselves, and they are prepared to be tyrants in the world. Thoughtful people, on the other hand, stand in contrast to both types of evildoers as resisters, nonparticipants, preserving their internal harmony.

Socrates, Arendt and Blücher believed, did not share the Platonic prejudice against opinion. His procedure was to question people's opinions and show them, in an intricate give-and-take, a dialogue, that they had neither considered their opinions (which they often discovered to be only relatively true) nor considered the consequences their opinions could have if used as a guide to action. The people Socrates engaged with sought knowledge and absolute truth, and thus were in a position to become either banally evil or wicked. Although Plato certainly presented Socrates as a truth-seeker, his goal was not truth; rather, he sought better-considered opinions and endless dialogue. He had discovered—

through his experience—that the internal dialogue he could conduct "between me and myself" could also be conducted with others.

But Arendt admitted candidly that Socrates had a "noble nature," with an *eros* for (love of) wisdom, beauty, and justice—all lovable, positive concepts. The consequence of such an eros was that he overlooked the unlovable concepts—evil, for instance—in his thinking, because he considered them simply an absence of the lovable concepts, rootless nothings. So he was protected from temptation or from the risk of following along with evildoers; he did not have to refuse to do evil. Rather, he announced on the basis of his experience the general conclusion that "no man does evil voluntarily." For Arendt, this meant that Socrates—nobly, but tragically—assumed that everyone, like himself, was capable of thinking and thus did not have to choose not to do evil. In effect, he could not understand the wicked people he saw voluntarily doing evil; certainly his dialogue with Alcibiades, a future traitor to their city, had no effect upon the man—Socrates was not able to turn him from his insane choice. How can thinking both confront evil and refuse it—refuse to live with a murderer? Or, to put the problem educationally or therapeutically, how does a person who does not have a noble nature acquire one and become able to confront evil? Can a person become a thinker who *confronts* evil and then refuses it *voluntarily?*

With this question, Arendt moved into the territory of the will. And here her beloved Greeks and her exemplary Socrates offered no guidance, for she realized that among the Greeks there was no conception of willing as a *free* faculty. The Greeks did have a concept of choice and a word for the faculty of choosing, *proairesis* (which the Christians called *liberum arbitrum,* "free choice"). For the Greeks, a choosing person chooses between preexisting possibilities—between right and wrong as preexisting courses or ends of action. But action, as Arendt understood it (and explored it in *The Human Condition*) is a new beginning, not a matter of following preexisting paths.

Just as reflective judging had its great explorer in Kant, and thinking had its great explorer in Socrates, willing, Arendt thought, had its pioneer in Saint Augustine, whom she called "the philosopher of the will." Augustine was able to explore the will because he was not hindered by two elements of thought that do not permit experiences of willing. First, if one thinks, as the Greeks and the Romans did, in terms of a cyclical theory of time, one cannot experience the future or true novelty—everything that comes from the future is felt to be the past coming around again. The idea that the future is not a road on which we march forward toward a known end but something that comes toward us, unknown and unknowable, neither a fate nor a necessity, was not a Greek or Roman concept. The Greeks and Romans believed in predetermined natures: you are born noble and good, or not, your nature was determined before your birth (some said in a previous life, some said by fate). As the Pre-Socratic philosopher Heraclitus put the matter summarily: "character is destiny." Second, if one thinks of action as a matter of choosing between one preexisting end and another preexisting end, one cannot conceptualize (even if one can experience and appreciate) the new beginning of action, which is set off by the free will.

Augustine, the fifth-century bishop of Hippo, in northern Africa, did not think within the framework of cyclical time, in which the future is the past coming around again. On the contrary, he thought that the future existed *only in our minds,* in our experience of it coming toward us. He also recognized conceptually that when we try to make a choice between one path and another; and then command ourselves to go one way or the other, we undergo a disconcerting, disharmonizing, experience: we command ourselves but immediately experience an I-will (*velle*) and an I-nill (*nolle*), a yes and a no. Saint Paul had also recognized this conflict but he understood it as a struggle between willing spirit and weak flesh. We become paralyzed because our bodily desires will not fall into line with our purer spirit—that is, because we are sinful creatures. And we must pray to God and await his grace to help us follow the right path. But Augustine, as he explains in *The Confessions,* understood the willing conflict differently. He had experienced a wild youth in which he was often unable to do what he thought he should—dedicate himself to the love of God, abjuring worldly pleasures— and he believed that the conflict lay in the will itself, not between spirit and flesh. This conflict in the will is the mark of its freedom; it is not a slavish faculty of obedience. God has endowed us with a *free* will, not an obedient one, not even one made to obey God's own commands. Therefore, to act we must love both God and this challenging, difficult gift. (I shall consider in a moment whether we must also both love our neighbors, starting with those nearest to us and then enlarging our circle, and love the concepts and courses of action that preserve such neighborly love.) Not grace from God, but love, "the weight of the soul," Augustine said, brings peace to the will.[18]

Augustine—and long after him the late-thirteenth-century theologian Duns Scotus, known as "the Subtle Doctor," whose beautiful passages on the transforming power of love Arendt also discusses—had a vision of (in Arendt's words) "Love as a kind of enduring and conflictless will." And she went on to elaborate what these Christians had taught her by suggesting that the "weight" or "gravity" of will transformed into love shapes a person's character, training the self to choose deliberately (with judgment) between different projects. But these projects are not natural givens; they are representational thought-things presented by imagination, such as justice—the very kind of thought-thing Socrates had loved without exploring the nature of that love. So Arendt claims, importantly, that people become just by loving (not only thinking about) justice. When we act, leaving the internal realm of the will and moving into the world to do this or that deed, we stop willing and lose that internal freedom in which I-will and I-nill are active and involved in the transformative power of love. But we act on the basis of our characters, which loving-willing has shaped. "Just as thinking prepares the self for the role of the spectator, willing fashions it into an 'enduring I' that directs all particular acts of volition. It creates the self's *character* and therefore was something understood as the *principium individuationis,* the source of a person's specific identity [as opposed to the person's talents and abilities, which are given by nature]."[19]

At the conclusion of her discussion of the will, Arendt did acknowledge that we lose the mental freedom of willing when we act, but what we gain is a shaped self; we gain the *who* we have to show in the world as we act, and that means we gain the possibility of *political* freedom, which, in turn, secures for us the conditions for freely thinking and willing. To explore what this claim implies, she turned to the "men of action" she took as exemplary—the American founding fathers. How did they, men with characters trained for action, understand and evaluate (judge) willing and its experience of the future? To answer that question, she made a brief but powerful excursion into an old theme: the hostility in the philosophical tradition toward anything that has to do with willing and action.

She began with a trenchant critique of Friedrich Nietzsche's criticism of the will. Nietzsche had railed against the limitation of the will, complaining that it cannot will backward, cannot undo the past, and he had tried to escape this reality, rather than—as Arendt herself did—facing it and exploring the human action of forgiving and through forgiveness being released from the past. Nietzsche's escape was to imagine that human beings have a "Will to Power" that can "transvalue all values," allowing them to *mentally* gain power over the past by criticizing it. He repudiated the power of action in favor of this delusional Will to Power, which was really an insanity of the will. From Arendt's point of view, Nietzsche's Will to Power was the most absurd chapter in the long history of philosophical hostility toward action and the desire to be freed from its unpredictability by the assertion of a solitary mental life divorced from the world, by sheer contemptus mundi.

Arendt's discussion of her second example of a modern philosopher who had turned away from action was much more personal and full of sadness. In great detail, with quotes and commentary, she explored Martin Heidegger's writings during and after the war in which he portrayed thinking as a "function of Being." Thinking was not for him a "dialogue between me and myself" but only a listening to Being. His was "a thinking that is not a willing." Recognizing only its own source, Being, as the determiner of human destinies, Heidegger's thinking denied that people in any way determine their own destinies. His thinking cut itself off decisively from willing, as though willing were the enemy of thinking. Here Heidegger was specifically repudiating Nietzsche's Will to Power but, further, he was repudiating the will altogether. For him the will was only a destructive faculty—a will to dominate. Such a conception could be seen as Heidegger's repudiation of his own disastrous entry into the political realm, his membership in the Nazi Party, but it carried the further implication that no one could enter political life without giving up the only kind of uncorrupted life there is, the life of the thinker. There was certainly no notion here that the will can constructively shape character, training a person to make choices, to act. It was this view of will and action that had led Arendt to diagnose him in a letter to Jaspers soon after the war as lacking character, "in the sense that he literally has none and certainly not a particularly bad one. At the same time, he lives in depths and with a passionateness that one can't easily forget. The distortion is intolerable." His "whole intricate and childish dishonesty" had "crept into his philosophizing," she lamented.[20]

Arendt was undoubtedly relieved to find on a close reading of her teacher's texts that during the war he had repudiated his time in the Nazi Party—although this does not excuse his never making a public recantation in language accessible to those unprepared to read his philosophical works. As I noted before, Arendt summarized his position in language that is much clearer than anything he ever wrote about it himself: "In Heidegger's understanding, the will to rule and to dominate is a kind of original sin, of which he found himself guilty when he tried to come to terms with his brief past in the Nazi movement."[21] But his mistake, from her point of view, was to assume that willing is willing to rule and to dominate. He failed to see that willing is at peace and nondominating when it is loving.

Nietzsche and Heidegger, in their different ways, judged action in the world as displeasing; to use the vocabulary of judging, they found it distasteful. Both of them experienced action as limiting, corrupting, and they were happy to remain within their minds. The American Revolution's men of action, to whom Arendt turned in the last pages of her "Willing" section, were men of a different sort, but they, too, were troubled by the will's difficult recoil and interior splitting, which is its freedom, troubled by action's unpredictability and by the fact that men acting can be men doing evil. Their worry, she suggested, is apparent in the way they tried—after they had emerged from the tutelage of the Church—to secure the secular political union they were founding by searching the annals of antiquity for "foundation legends," stories of how exemplary acts of liberation could lead, after a period of transition, to a good and stable new order. Their point of reference became the story of Rome's founding as told in Virgil's *Aeneid,* in which Rome is imagined as a refounding of Troy.

Without a foundation image from the past to guide them into the future, actors can become unable to leave the inner freedom of willing something to venture into acting in the world. From ancient times through Marx, men of action have been prone to look for an ancient past that they could re-create as the radiant future. Some have even looked further back, to a pastoral pre-political fairy-tale world, a Golden Age (in Marx's terms, a world before the division of labor and the emergence of classes). These images helped them face the unknown future.

After she had explored the use the American founders made of their guiding foundation legend, Arendt admitted, in the close of her "Willing" section, that she had come to an impasse.

> When we directed our attention to men of action, hoping to find in them a notion of freedom purged of the perplexities caused for men's minds by the reflexivity of mental activities—the inevitable recoil on itself of the willing ego—we hoped for more than we finally achieved. The abyss of pure spontaneity, which in the foundation legends is bridged by the hiatus between liberation and the constitution of freedom, was covered up by the device, typical of the Occidental tradition (the only tradition where freedom has always been the *raison d'être* of all politics) of understanding the new as an improved re-statement of the old. In its original integrity freedom survived in political theory—i.e., theory conceived for the purpose of political action—only in utopian and unfounded promises of a final "realm of freedom" that, in its Marxian version, at any rate, would indeed spell the "end of all things," a sempiternal peace in which all specifically human activities would wither away.

Could there be a political theory in which "the abyss of pure spontaneity," freedom in its "original integrity," did not disappear? As she considered the displeasure people feel about their freedom, which she considered unavoidably theirs by virtue of the fact of their having been born for being new beginnings, and how they try to escape or control it, Arendt suggested that there was no way to understand this displeasure except "by an appeal to another mental faculty, no less mysterious than the faculty of beginning, the faculty of judgment, an analysis of which at least may tell us what is involved in our pleasures and displeasures."[22]

And it was just this analysis of the faculty of judgment that she did not live to write. But we can see what she was looking for—the final step in the story of the interrelations of the activities of thinking, willing, and judging, with their checks and balances. Thinking gives judging and willing thought-things for them to choose and to judge; willing gives thinking and judging the self's character as the basis for thinking's dialogue and judging's impartiality, disinterestedness, and communicability. And what does judging, which is pleased or displeased, give? To thinking: the relatedness to others that thinking in its solitude does not have, the enlarged mentality. To willing: a public realm constituted by critics and spectators into which it sends its volitions for their pleasure or displeasure, discussion and disputation. Judging helps constitute the public realm, the realm of *political* freedom without which no one would be safe to retire for thinking freely and no one's free acts would be checked and humanized by being discussed. Arendt did not look for a political theory to guide action, she looked for judges—all the citizens—who would keep action from self-destruction and from destroying the political realm in which it is possible. Action that destroys the conditions of its own possibility is, in her theory, evil.

. . .

The Life of the Mind, with its intricate and complicated analyses of mental experiences and concepts for those experiences, and its long excursions into the history of philosophy, is certainly no field manual, nor is it a primer. But it does share with *The Origins of Totalitarianism* and *The Human Condition* the characteristic that if you use it as a lens you can come to the heart of the mental dilemmas of our time. Let us turn its lens on three questions that have application for our own times: Is there a moral philosophy that people of diverse moral traditions might be persuaded to agree upon? How can the love that harmonizes the will be understood politically? And how can we imagine the cosmopolitan public realm of critics and spectators?

Moral philosophy in the West, with its roots in Greek *ethike* and Judeo-Christian law, has always involved objective and subjective divisions: study of moral customs, norms, or laws and study of character (the word *character,* too, comes from the Greek, and refers to the impress a stylus makes upon a clay tablet, metaphorically suggesting that we are as we have been written upon). Moral philosophy traditionally asked, "What is the Good?" "And what is the character of the one able to know and do good?" Some moral philosophers have looked to nature for norms that naturally guide people; some have looked to a transcendent realm, a divine, grounding or giving the moral law; some have said that the law or the norms are immediately evident to anyone with a capacity for faith or a reasoning mind or a feeling heart; some have emphasized the need for moral education and character-shaping discipline. Kant, heir to centuries of philosophical variants on these themes, heroically appealed to neither nature nor the divine but to the principle that guides all humans, universal reason's own categorical imperative: to do the right thing, people need only act so that their action could be formulated as a universal law.

But Arendt thought, as I indicated, that Kant's effort was not radical enough, and did not get to the core of moral philosophy. For her that core could be seen most clearly in the example of Socrates, and in the examples of those like Jaspers and Blücher who had learned from his example. This Socratic way of thinking could give exemplary guidance (not rules) to the survivors of a time when, she argued, all norms and laws, including Kant's imperative—the whole Western moral philosophical tradition— simply collapsed. "We—at least the older ones among us—have witnessed the total collapse of all established moral standards in public and private life during the nineteen-thirties and forties, not only (as is now usually assumed) in Hitler's Germany but also in Stalin's Russia."[23]

The true radicality of Arendt's own moral philosophizing was that, steadfastly staring at the evidence of this collapse, she did not do what most witnesses then and most people since have done: call for a moral restoration, a return to an old order. She did not ask, "What is the Good?" Instead, she insisted that in a crisis a truly thinking person will not look for rules or laws but will say, "I must be true to myself. I must not do anything that I cannot live with, that I cannot bear to remember." That "standard of the self" has been, she claimed, the "almost unanimous assumption of moral philosophy throughout the centuries." But that claim, the recognition of this assumption as unanimous, was unique to Arendt. Most philosophers, including Kant, have been unable to assume this standard of the self, much less explore it. The assumption did not please them, they did not approve it— to speak in the language of reflective judgment—and they felt fearfully compelled to abandon it for supposedly objective standards, rules, and laws. They could not say with Shakespeare, "To thine own self be true, and thou canst not then be false to any man." Arendt wanted to recover the standard of the self, to reassert it clearly and forcefully, and to explore its consequences: "Morality concerns the individual in his singularity. The criterion of right and wrong, the answer to the question what ought I to do? depends in the last analysis neither on habits and customs, which I share with those around me, nor on a command of either divine or human origin, but on what I decide with regard to myself. In other words, I cannot do certain things because having done them I can no longer be able to live with myself."[24] Morality is being faithful to—not forgetting—what was and is true in oneself and for oneself.

Human beings are able to hold internal dialogues when they are provoked into thinking by a worldly event or something they themselves have done or might do; they are provoked into telling their experience to themselves "as a kind of story, preparing it in this way for its subsequent communication to others" and preparing it in this way to be remembered. Those who think in this internal, dialogic way are prepared to consult others who also think in this way and are thus prepared to judge reflectively; they are prepared to submit their thinking to a community of spectators with enlarged mentality. Those who do not have this ability of thinking and then judging will do wrong in action; further, Arendt said, "to do wrong is to spoil this ability."[25]

The implication of this radical statement for understanding moral character is startling. A person who does wrong, and thereby spoils his or her ability to think—to conduct an internal dialogue, to remember the past—can *destroy his or her moral character.* "For human beings thinking of past matters means moving in the dimension of depth, striking roots and thus stabilizing themselves, so as not to be swept away by whatever may occur—the Zeitgeist or History or simple temptation." A person who is not thus stabilized, as Heidegger (who rejected the idea of thinking as dialogue) was not, has no *moral* character. Or, as she put it (using here the term *moral personality* rather than *character*), we could say, "In the process of thought . . . I explicitly constitute myself a person, and I shall remain one to the extent that I am capable of such constitution *ever again and anew* [emphasis added]. If this is what we commonly call [moral] personality, and it has nothing to do with gifts and intelligence, [then] it is the simple almost automatic result of thoughtfulness."[26]

I think that in these passages Arendt made a persuasive case for her claim that the standard of the self is the experiential core of morality, but I also think that she did not take her case far enough. She made the claim in the "Thinking" section of her last book but did not revisit it after she had written the "Willing" section and prepared her lectures for the "Judging" section. Considering her own emphasis on the interrelatedness of the mental faculties, it does not seem that thinking alone can be the seat and source of morality, or that the thinking ego is the self for the standard of the self. She taught us to consider the self as a character shaped by lovingly related willing (an "enduring I") and the enlarged mentality of judging, not by thinking alone. This character shaped by willing is trained not to support volitions that destroy its individuality, its singularity, or its relatedness. The standard of the undivided self is also upheld by the reflectively judging I, which does not judge alone, but only in relation to others, in enlarged mentality.

People who are deciding not to live with a murderer—or a liar, or a thief—are also making judgments about what to do, which course of action to will, especially what to do in their relations with others. They often consult trusted others as they make their decisions. They frame the standard of the self not just in the "do-not-do-this" terms of solitary thinking but through formulations from the domains of willing and judging as well. They say with the Christians, to take an example from the domain of the will, "Do unto others as you would have others do unto you," or, in the more profound form that the Chinese sage Confucius found for this maxim (and offered to his students in the *Analects*): "What you do not want done to yourself, do not hand out to others." The Confucian maxim suggests that you refrain from doing the harm to others that you have experienced and remembered (or can imagine experiencing by consulting the experience of others); it suggests that you do not first look to the future ("do unto others") but draw upon your past experience as an example—using your reflective judgment—and then refrain from recycling past harm in the future. It seems to me that even people who pray for divine guidance use this standard of the thinking-willing-judging self in relation to others; and variant formulations of the Christian and Confucian maxims can be found in all the religions descended from the Axial Age religions. Indeed, if Kant's categorical imperative were framed in less legalistic, less imperative, and less categorical terms, it could escape Arendt's persuasive critique of it and be similar to the commonsensical Confucian standard of the self; it could say, "Deeds you do not want done to you, try not to do to any member of the human tribe, for you will be harmed again, and you will harm, if these deeds become the norm."

I am persuaded that the standard of the self is the core of morality, and it pleases me (pleases my judging I) that this is so, for it seems to me that this standard could be persuasive to people of any moral-religious tradition. I wonder how you judge the matter.

An anthology on love collected from the works of philosophers around the world probably would not include anything by Hannah Arendt. She wrote no essay or treatise called "On Love." In *The Life of the Mind*'s "Willing" section, she did, as we have seen, claim that love heals the division in the will (the will's I-will and I-nill) that shows its freedom. But she did not elaborate on love there, nor did she connect her insight to the discussion of the American men of action, the founding fathers, who worried about whether their unpredictable actions would lead to a new constitution, and resorted to a foundation legend for their new Rome. Both the elaboration on love and the missing connection, however, can be found in *The Human Condition*.

For Arendt, love is intrinsically unworldly; that is, it exists only in the private sphere as love between two persons or as familial love. Publicity destroys it (as those who seek to celebrate their love in the public realm of the news media soon enough discover). In *The Human Condition* Arendt had noted that Augustine had suggested that love could and should be a political principle for Christian communities, but he had assumed that those communities would be unworldly. In fact, the little communities that grew up on his principles, such as the monastic communities of the Middle Ages, though unworldly, were hardly the loving communities Augustine had envisioned or Saint Francis had come closer to instituting. The monastic orders had resorted to rules and regulations, often quite authoritarian ones. Love of goodness, too, as Jesus of Nazareth had taught, is perverted as soon as it makes an appearance in the world or is held up as a political principle. It should remain hidden, even to those who do good deeds—the left hand, he taught, should not know what the right hand is doing; our reward will come only from God. Similarly, in the Jewish tradition, God was willing to save the world for the sake of the thirty-six righteous men in it, who were known to no one, least of all themselves.[27]

In *The Human Condition,* Arendt had agreed with Machiavelli (and his Greek and Roman sources) that the criterion by which action should be judged is greatness, not goodness: "Goodness that comes out of hiding and assumes a public role is no longer goodness, but corrupt in its own terms and will carry its own corruption wherever it goes." (Although she did allow that goodness, when it appears in deeds and is thus corrupt, "may still be useful as an act of organized charity or an act of solidarity.")[28] Living as we do in a historical moment when religious ideologues of all sorts have forgotten the lessons about corruption of the Christian Middle Ages that Machiavelli tried to recall for both the church and the states of his time, we can give new ears to Arendt's effort to be modernly Machiavellian. Nonetheless, it is important to remember her warning about the corruption of goodness, about the way it can become simply a rationalization for violence, such as now emanates from clashing religious adherents.

But what of Arendt's claim that people become just by loving justice? The training of the just—that is, judicious—character also takes place in private. Love as "the weight of the soul" is experienced internally, on the basis of love between persons: love between parents and children and love between adults. (Lovers, in Arendt's understanding, remain unworldly in their love until they "insert a new world into the existing world" by producing a child, who is "representative of the world" and must be loved and provided for there as a new beginning.)[29] Characters trained by love do recommit to the world and act in the public realm: love's therapy has an indirect effect. At the least, a person whose character has been trained by love will try to preserve the common world or the public realm in which character can be manifest, in which *who* a person is can make an appearance. A person whose character has been trained by love will want to preserve the world as a place where acts that ultimately flow from love— acts of solidarity, acts of mutual pledging—can exist.

This effort at preservation is what Arendt called respect, as we noted before in our consideration of promise making as the political capacity for securing the future. As she wrote in *The Human Condition,* "Respect, not unlike the Aristotelian *philia politike,* is a kind of 'friendship' without intimacy and without closeness; it is a regard for the person from the distance which the space of the world puts between us."[30] The space between us is the space that allows us to appreciate another person's point of view as different from our own. It allows us to be spectators—judges—and to enjoy in respectful friendship the differences among our judgments and opinions as well as to make the promises in which our differences are reconciled for the sake of political life.

Even in its unfinished state, Arendt's *Life of the Mind* can be experienced as her response to the example of Socrates' thinking, Saint Augustine's willing, and Kant's reflective judging, each of which she both learned from and criticized. She was looking for a thinking that does not depend upon a noble nature but can lead to a moral resistance to evildoing; a willing that is healed by love and leads to respectful volitions or actions, but does not make love a political principle; a judging that does not surrender its reflectivity to imperatives. Hers was a philosophical project of great complexity, a vast integration of exemplary teachings that she made on the basis of her own experience, in and for her own historical context. Using his own terms, Heinrich Blücher had spoken of these three areas of human and humane activity that must be interrelated, developing together: "philosophy, or the relation of man to himself, erotics, or the relation of man to man, and politics, or the relation of man to mankind."[31]

Blücher admitted that the relation of man to mankind is "the hardest" sphere—as judging is the most difficult, although the most pleasing, activity to engage in. In the life of the mind, it requires both the steadfastness to face reality, especially unprecedented reality, and the Kantian enlarged mentality and willingness not to impose one's own viewpoint on others; in politics, it requires an understanding of the unity of humankind and a renunciation of the hegemony of one's own group or the sovereignty of one's own state. In his *Origin and Goal of History,* as he was imagining a possible future world order of federated states, Jaspers had drawn the political conclusion clearly:

> Where a sovereignty remains that is not that of mankind as a whole, there also remains a source of unfreedom; for it [state sovereignty] must assert itself as force against force. The organization of force, conquest[,] and empire-building by conquest, lead to dictatorship, even if the starting point was free democracy. So it happened in Rome in the transition from the Republic to Caesarism. So the French Revolution changed into the dictatorship of Napoleon. Democracy that conquers abandons itself. Democracy that lives on good terms with others lays the foundations for the union of all with equal rights. The demand for full sovereignty is rooted in the energy of self-assertion destitute of communication. In the [European] age of absolutism, when the concept of sovereignty was defined, the consequences were ruthlessly made conscious in word and deed.[32]

Like Jaspers, Arendt had understood that excluding any individual from the enlarged mentality of others' judgments contributes to the exclusion of individuals and groups from humankind. Sovereignty of mind, mental lack of democracy, contributes to political sovereignty, which is "not that of mankind as a whole." The removal of people from our judging consideration contributes to the removal of them from humanity and human history. And being considerate of them contributes to their being included. From the time of *The Origins of Totalitarianism* Arendt had understood enlarged mentality as the preventative for thoughtless and thus judgmentless crimes against humanity. She had always written out of solidarity with the victims of such crimes, with the conviction that telling their story for the sake of the future was her life task. So she had concluded the first edition of *The Origins of Totalitarianism* with these words about the usefulness of the story she had told in her book—words that still illuminate why Arendt matters.

> Only a consciously planned beginning of history, only a consciously devised new polity, will eventually be able to reintegrate those who in ever increasing numbers are being expelled from humanity and severed from the human condition. The recognition of a crime against humanity will, by itself, achieve neither liberty nor justice, for these are the concern of the daily life of all citizens; it can only secure the participation of all in the strife. The concept of human rights can only be meaningful if they are redefined as a right to the human condition itself, which depends upon belonging to some human community, the right never to be dependent on some inborn human dignity which *de facto,* aside from its guarantee by fellow-men, not only does not exist but is the last and most arrogant myth we have invented in all our long history. The Rights of Man can be implemented only if they become the prepolitical foundation of a new polity, the prelegal basis of a new legal structure, the, so to speak, prehistorical fundament from which the history of mankind will derive its essential meaning. . . .
>
> In the meantime, it may have been useful to find the origin, and to contemplate the forms, of those new movements which pretend to have discovered the solutions to our problems, and whose fantas-

tic claims to having founded thousand year empires and Messianic ages are believed, despite all evidence to the contrary, because they respond, albeit in a radically destructive way, to the terrible challenges of the century. This certainly cannot establish a new law on earth, but it is one way toward a new form or universal solidarity.

For those who were expelled from humanity and from human history and thereby deprived of their human condition need the solidarity of all men to assure them of their rightful place in "man's enduring chronicle." At least we can cry out to each one of those who rightly is in despair: "Do thy self no harm; for we are all here." (Acts, 16:28).[33]

notes

Unless otherwise identified, all works are by Hannah Arendt.

introduction

1. *Eichmann in Jerusalem,* pp. 93, 95.

2. Ibid., p. 106.

3. *The Human Condition,* "Prologue," p. 6.

4. *Eichmann in Jerusalem,* p. 27.

5. *Men in Dark Times,* "Preface," p. ix.

6. Ibid., "On Humanity in Dark Times, p. 11.

7. Ibid., "Karl Jaspers: A Laudatio," p. 77.

8. Ibid., "Preface," p. ix.

9. *Crises of the Republic,* "Lying in Politics: Reflections on the Pentagon Papers," sect. 1, p. 13.

10. See *Between Past and Future,* "Tradition and the Modern Age."

11. *Men in Dark Times,* "On Humanity in Dark Times," p. 20.

12. Immanuel Kant, *The Critique of Pure Reason,* B 172–173, cited in Arendt, *Responsibility and Judgment,* "Some Questions of Moral Philosophy," p. 137.

13. *Men in Dark Times,* "Karl Jaspers: A Laudatio," p. 78.

14. Elżbieta Ettinger, *Hannah Arendt/Martin Heidegger* (New Haven: Yale University Press, 1995). I discuss Ettinger's book in detail in the new introduction to my *Hannah Arendt: For Love of the World,* 2d ed. (New Haven: Yale University Press, 2004).

15. Ettinger, *Arendt/Heidegger,* pp. 42, 78, 74, 79.

16. Letter of March 11, 1949, *Arendt/Jaspers Correspondence,* p. 133.

17. *Essays in Understanding,* "The Image of Hell," p. 201. Jaspers chronicled his decision to break with Heidegger in an autobiographical essay, which has recently been published in German, as have the letters between Jaspers and Heidegger. For a selection these letters in English, see *Karl Jaspers: Basic Philosophical Writings,* ed. E. Ehrlich, L. H. Ehrlich, and G. Pepper (Atlantic Highlands, N.J.: Humanities Press International, 1994).

18. *The Life of the Mind,* pt. 2, p. 173.

19. *Eichmann in Jerusalem,* p. 298.

20. *Rahel Varnhagen,* p. 35.

21. Ibid., p. 8.

22. *Essays in Understanding,* "What Is Existential Philosophy?" p. 187.

one. *The Origins of Totalitaranism*
and the Twenty-first Century

1. *Men in Dark Times,* "On Humanity in Dark Times," p. 24.

2. Recommended reading for today is Morgenthau's "We Are Deluding Ourselves in Vietnam, *New York Times Magazine,* April 18, 1965, a piece that had great impact on Arendt's thoughts about American leaders and their dedication to images, especially Morgenthau's contention, "The Government fashions an imaginary world that pleases it, and then comes to believe in the reality of that world and acts as though it were real."

3. *Essays in Understanding,* "What Remains? The Language Remains. A Conversation with Gunther Gaus," p. 13. See also Elisabeth Young-Bruehl, *For Love of the World,* 2d ed. (New Haven: Yale University Press, 2004), p. 185.

4. Letter of September 4, 1947, *Arendt/Jaspers Correspondence,* p. 98.

5. *Origins of Totalitarianism,* pp. 631–632.

6. Ibid., p. xxvii.

7. "The Aftermath of Nazi Rule" is reprinted in *Essays in Understanding,* 248–269.

8. *Between Past and Future,* "What Is Authority?" pp. 95, 99.

9. *Responsibility and Judgment,* "*The Deputy:* Guilt by Silence?" pp. 214–226.

10. *The Life of the Mind,* pt. 1, p. 5.

11. *The Origins of Totalitarianism,* "Ideology and Terror," p. 593.

12. *Essays in Understanding,* "Religion and Politics," p. 379.

13. Ibid., p. 373.

14. *The Promise of Politics,* "Introduction into Politics," p. 200.

15. See *New York Times,* December 15, 2005, p. A-21.

16. *The Origins of Totalitarianism,* "Concluding Remarks," p . 623.

17. Ibid., p. 626.

18. Ibid., p. 631.

19. See Bruce Lawrence, ed., *Messages to the World: The Statements of Osama bin Laden* (New York: Verso, 2006).

two.   *The Human Condition* and Actions That Matter

1. Letter of August 6, 1955, *Arendt/Jaspers Correspondence,* p. 264.

2. *The Human Condition,* "Prologue," p. 6.

3. Ibid., pt. 1, sec. 1, p. 9.

4. Ibid., pt. 2, sec. 4, p. 24.

5. Ibid., pt. 1, sec. 2, p. 14.

6. *On Revolution,* p. 318*n*1.

7. Ibid., p. 280.

8. *Men in Dark Times,* "Karl Jaspers: A Laudatio," p. 75.

9. *The Human Condition,* pt. 5, sec. 28, p. 184.

10. *Men in Dark Times,* "On Humanity in Dark Times," p. 20.

11. Ibid., p. 21.

12. *The Human Condition,* pt. 5, sec. 28, p. 180.

13. The distinction is made in *The Human Condition* and in more detail later in *On Violence.*

14. See Richard Drayton, "Shock, Awe and Hobbes Have Back-Fired on America's Neocons," *Guardian,* December 28, 2005.

15. *On Revolution,* p. 174.

16. See Danny Postel, "Noble Lies and Perpetual War," on www.open democracy, October 15, 2003, which includes a bibliography of current articles on Strauss.

17. Thomas Hobbes, *Leviathan* (New York: Penguin, 1985), bk. 13.

18. Ibid., bks. 29, 21.

19. *Essays in Understanding,* "The Threat of Conformism," p. 427.

20. *The Human Condition,* pt. 5, sec. 33, p. 215.

21. Ibid., p. 214.

22. Ibid., pp. 215, 362*n*80.

23. Ibid., p. 216.

24. Ibid., pt. p. 217.

25. Luke 7:47; *The Human Condition,* pt. 5, sec. 33, p. 218.

26. *Men in Dark Times,* "Angelo Giuseppe Roncalli: A Christian on St. Peter's Chair from 1958 to 1963," pp. 57–70.

27. *Eichmann in Jerusalem,* p. 289.

28. Ibid., p. 272.

29. Martin Luther King, "Loving Your Enemies," sermon delivered to the Dexter Avenue Baptist Church, Montgomery, Alabama, Christmas 1957.

30. Desmond Tutu, *No Future Without Forgiveness* (New York: Doubleday, 1999), p. 23.

31. Pumla Gobodo-Madikizela, *A Human Being Died That Night* (New York: Houghton Mifflin, 2003), p. 15.

32. Tutu, *No Future Without Forgiveness,* p. 272.

33. Ibid., p. 279.

34. Ibid., p. 30.

35. *The Human Condition,* pt. 5, sec. 34, p. 219.

36. *The Human Condition,* pt. 5, sec. 34, p. 217.

37. *Crises of the Republic,* "Civil Disobedience," p. 66.

38. *On Revolution,* pp. 223, 230, 176.

39. *On Revolution,* p. 154.

40. Ibid., p. 174.

41. Ibid., p. 239.

42. Ibid., p. 278.

43. *Crises of the Republic,* p. 89.

44. *On Revolution,* p. 282.

45. Letter of September 2, 1968, *Within Four Walls,* p. 388.

46. Adam Michnik, *Letters from Prison and Other Essays,* trans. Maya Latynski (Berkeley: University of California Press, 1985); Arendt, *On Violence,* p. 80.

47. My thanks to Elzbieta Matynia of the New School for this information, which will be discussed in her forthcoming book.

48. Václav Havel, "The Power of the Powerless," in Havel et al., *The Power of the Powerless: Citizens Against the State in Central-Eastern Europe* (Armonk, N.Y.: M. E. Sharpe, 1985).

49. Foreword to Karl Jaspers, *The Future of Germany* (Chicago: University of Chicago Press, 1967), p. v.

50. Ibid., p. ix.

51. Foreword to Jaspers, *Future of Germany,* p. viii, quoting Jaspers.

52. Cohn-Bendit was interviewed about his relationship with Arendt by *Die Welt* on December 3, 2005; English translation at www.signand sight.com/features/510.html.

53. *On Violence,* pp. 17–18.

54. *Essays in Understanding,* "The Threat of Conformism," p. 427.

55. See *The Human Condition,* pt. 6, sec. 45, p. 295.

56. Ibid., "Prologue," p. 4.

57. *Responsibility and Judgment,* "Home to Roost," pp. 257–275.

58. Ibid., p. 264.

59. *Crises of the Republic,* "Lying in Politics," p. 34.

three.   Thinking About *The Life of the Mind*

1. *Origins of Totalitarianism,* "Preface," p. xxvi.

2. Letter of December 21, 1968, *Between Friends,* p.230; *On Revolution,* p. 232.

3. Letter of August 29, 1957, *Arendt/Jaspers Correspondence,* p. 318.

4. *Responsibility and Judgment,* "Some Questions of Moral Philosophy," p. 141, (referring to Kant's *Anthropology from a Pragmatic Point of View*).

5. See *The Life of the Mind,* pt. 2, p. 257.

6. *Responsibility and Judgment,* "Some Questions of Moral Philosophy," p. 137, quoting Kant.

7. *The Life of the Mind,* pt. 2, pp. 263, 268.

8. Ibid., p. 263.

9. *The Promise of Politics,* "Socrates," p. 13.

10. Michel de Montaigne, "Of Presumption," *The Complete Essays of Montaigne,* trans. Donald Frame (Stanford: Stanford University Press, 1958), p. 499.

11. *The Promise of Politics,* "Introduction into Politics," p. 168.

12. Montaigne, "Of Presumption," p. 499.

13. Michel de Montaigne, "Of Cannibals," *Complete Essays of Montaigne,* p. 155.

14. *The Life of the Mind,* pt. 2, p. 202.

15. *On Revolution,* p. 230.

16. *The Life of the Mind,* pt. 1, p. 185.

17. Ibid., pp. 190–191.

18. Ibid., pt. 2, p. 95.

19. Ibid., p. 195.

20. Letter of September 29, 1949, *Arendt/Jaspers Correspondence,* p. 142.

21. *The Life of the Mind,* pt. 2, p. 173.

22. Ibid., p. 216.

23. *Responsibility and Judgment,* "Some Questions of Moral Philosophy," p. 52.

24. *The Life of the Mind,* pt. 1, pp. 102, 97.

25. Ibid., pt. 2, p. 94.

26. *Responsibility and Judgment,* "Some Questions of Moral Philosophy," p. 95.

27. *The Human Condition,* pt. 2, sec. 10, pp. 66–68.

28. Ibid., p. 69.

29. Ibid., pt. 5, sec. 33, p. 218.

30. Ibid.

31. *Within Four Walls,* "A Lecture from the Common Course," p. 397.

32. Karl Jaspers, *The Origin and Goal of History* (New York: Routledge and Kegan Paul, 1953; German original, 1949), p. 197.

33. *The Origins of Totalitarianism,* pp. 631–632.

works by hannah arendt

Hannah Arendt's books exist in many English editions, from many different publishers, and they have been widely translated. In my notes I cite the latest editions or indicate the sections, chapters, or essays rather than citing only the page numbers so that quotations can be located using any edition. The works below are listed in order of English-language publication where such exists.

The Origins of Totalitarianism [1951]. Rev. ed.; New York: Schocken, 2004. (Includes all the prefaces and additions from the 1958, 1968, and 1972 editions.)

The Human Condition. Chicago: University of Chicago Press, 1958.

Rahel Varnhagen: The Life of a Jewess [1958]. Complete ed.; Ed. Liliane Weissberg. Baltimore: Johns Hopkins University Press, 1997.

Between Past and Future: Six Exercises in Political Thought. New York: Viking, 1961. (Two more essays were added in 1968; a new edition is due in 2006.)

On Revolution. New York: Viking, 1963. (A new edition is due in 2006.)

Eichmann in Jerusalem: A Report on the Banality of Evil [1963]. Rev. ed.: New York: Viking, 1968. (A new edition is in preparation.)

Men in Dark Times. New York: Harcourt, Brace and World, 1968.

On Violence. New York: Harcourt, Brace and World, 1970. (Also included in *Crises of the Republic.*)

Crises of the Republic. New York: Harcourt Brace Jovanovich, 1972.

The Life of the Mind. Ed. Mary McCarthy. 2 vols. New York: Harcourt Brace Jovanovich, 1978.

Hannah Arendt/Karl Jaspers Correspondence, 1926–1969. Ed. Lotte Kohler and Hans Saner. New York: Harcourt Brace Jovanovich, 1992.

Essays in Understanding, 1930–1954. Ed. Jerome Kohn. New York: Harcourt, Brace, 1994. Paperback ed.; New York: Schocken, 2005.

Between Friends: The Correspondence of Hannah Arendt and Mary McCarthy, 1949–1975. Ed. Carol Brightman. New York: Harcourt, Brace, 1995.

Hannah Arendt and Kurt Blumenfeld. *". . . in keinem Besitz verwuzelt": Die Korresponenz.* Ed. Ingeborg Nordmann and Iris Pilling. Hamburg: Rotbuch, 1995.

Within Four Walls: The Correspondence Between Hannah Arendt and Heinrich Blücher, 1936–1968. Ed. Lotte Kohler. New York: Harcourt, 1996.

Hannah Arendt and Hermann Broch. *Briefwechsel 1946 bis 1951.* Ed. Paul Michale Lutzler. Frankfurt am Main: Judischer Verlag/Suhrkamp, 1996.

Responsibility and Judgment. Ed. Jerome Kohn. New York: Schocken, 2003.

Hannah Arendt and Martin Heidegger. *Letters, 1925–1975.* Ed. Ursula Ludz. New York: Harcourt, 2004.

The Promise of Politics. Ed. Jerome Kohn. New York: Schocken, 2005.

acknowledgments

Thanks to Ileene Smith, my editor at Yale University Press; Susan Laity, the manuscript editor; and their colleagues for careful work on this book and for the honor of their choosing it to launch their "Why X Matters" series. My *Hannah Arendt: For Love of the World* was also published by Yale, and I appreciate the care given the biography, too, over the years since my friend and editor Maureen MacGrogan worked with me on the first edition in 1982 (a second edition appeared in 2004). Along with Jerome Kohn, whose contribution to this book is chronicled in it, good friends read all or parts of this manuscript: Darlene Arendt, Dominique Browning, Micah Burch, Jonathan Schell, Lois and Ernest Sutton (my parents), and Eva von Redecker. I am grateful that Dan Frank, formerly my student, is now Arendt's publisher at Schocken Books, thanks to the good offices of Georges Borchardt, who has been for almost twenty-five years my trusted literary agent. It is my pleasure to dedicate this book to Christine Dunbar, M.D., F.R.C.P.[C]. *Amor magnus doctor est* (Saint Augustine).

index